R.I. Walters' Wine Guide
to Australian Wine

National Library of Australia Cataloguing-in-Publication data:

Walters, Robert I.
 R.I. Walters' wine guide to Australian wines
 Bibliography.
 Includes index.
 ISBN 1-875655 70 0

 1. Wine and wine making – Australia. 1. Title. II. Title: Wine guide to Australian wines.

641.220994

Publisher: Richard Carroll
Author: Robert I. Walters
Art Director: Maria Centorino - Terraplane Press
Graphic Icons: Robyn Macready
Photo - Illustrations: Edwina White

R&R Publishing Pty Ltd
PO Box 63
Terrey Hills NSW 2084

FOREWORD

I don't know Robert Walters but my daughter Sally tells me he's a good chap. He is also a considerable wine scholar with a definite point of view. His experience in the wine industry, both in corporate marketing and retail, has driven him to compile a guide that offers wine buyers access to the information required to make informed decisions.

Since the question I have been asked most often throughout my career is "What wine do you recommend?" I have some sympathy for such a project. For those who ask this question are often unaware of the counter-questions that such enquiries lead to: "What styles of wine do you like?", "What country or region?", "What grape variety?", "How much would you like to pay?"

The first Wine Australia exposition proved beyond doubt that there is a great demand for wine knowledge, particularly amongst young wine lovers. It may even be fair to say that the younger generations have been largely ignored by certain sections of the wine industry. It is certainly important that wine drinkers of all ages learn to use wine wisely, moderately, with food and amongst friends, for their greater enjoyment.

Robert Walters has sought to address this issue by structuring his book in such a way that it is accessible to the beginner, the young wine lover, and equally those, already initiated, who would like to learn more about this fascinating subject without becoming wine sages or, Bacchus forbid, wine bores.

May the Gods bless this book and all those who drink from its pages.

— Len Evans OBE

CONTENTS

INSTANT WINE KNOWLEDGE

A Quick Demystification Of Wine Pg 11
Sorting Out The Wine Snobs Pg 11
How To Taste Wine As Though You Were An Expert Pg 12
How The Wine Trade Functions And
The Value Of A Good Retailer Pg 14
Decanting Wine Pg 16
A Whinge About Our Restaurants Pg 18
The Aging Of Wine Pg 20
Oaky Dokey? Oak & Its Effect On Wine Pg 22
How Wine Is Made (Diagram Format) Pg 24
Wine Additives: The 'Preservatives' Myth Pg 26
Understanding Australian Wine Labels Pg 28

WHICH REGION ?

Wine Blending & The Meaning Of Region Pg 31

An alphabetic listing of what each region, as listed on wine labels, has to offer the wine buyer. In short, what each region does best. Pg 33

GRAPE VARIETIES AND OTHER WINE TITLES

A glossary of the many titles that appear on wine labels, from Classic Dry White to Cabernet Sauvignon.
What the wine buyer can expect from these wines and what regions offer the best examples. Pg 45

FOOD & WINE

An extensive listing of food and wine matchings. Pg 61

WHICH WINE?

In this section of the guide, over three hundred wines are reviewed under their appropriate wine-style headings. This enables you, the reader, to choose your wines, not only in reference to quality, but also with regard to the food you will be eating, and, more importantly, the style of wine you are in the mood to drink. Greatest vintages, aging potential, and information about how the wine was made are also given.

RED WINES FOR HEROES:
Massively rich and tannic red wines. Enormous weight of viscous, mouth coating fruit and inky, astringent tannins Pg 71

FULL BODIED REDS:
Full flavoured reds with good weight of fruit and firm tannins. Pg 79

ELEGANT REDS:
Soft and graceful red wines that show immaculate balance and an extra level of refinements. Pg 101

PINOT NOIR:
Not as heavy as the red wines previously listed, these are none the less fleshy reds with good intensity of flavour Pg 123

LIGHT REDS AND ROSE:
Thirst quenching reds with delicious berry characters & crisp acidity. Pg133

CRISP & DRY WHITES:
Austere in flavour with crisp acid and a streak of herbaceousness. Pg 137

DRY RIESLINGS:
Packed with citrus/floral characters and zesty acidity. Pg 143

PERFUMED & DRY - THE AROMATICS:
Abundant flavours of gooseberry, tropical fruits, along with a dry, grassy finish. Pg 151

FULL FLAVOURED, DRY WHITES with oak influence:
These wines range from crisp, and restrained in flavour, to super rich, powerhouses of oak and viscous fruit. Pg 159

SWEET & STICKY, THE DESSERT WINES:
Rich and concentrated, sweet wines that show ripe apricot and spice aromas and flavours. Pg 179

TOKAYS (soon to have a name change) AND MUSCATS:
Raisiny, chocolaty Muscats and Tokays full of toffee and sweet, cold tea flavours. Pg 186

SPARKLING WINES:
Not only for celebration, ideal pre-dinner or with food. Pg 189

GLOSSARY OF WINE-MAKING & TASTING TERMS
An extensive listing of wine terms used both in this guide and throughout wine literature. Pg 199

INDEX
A complete index of the wines listed in the "Which Wines" Section. Pg 212

DEDICATION

This book is dedicated to the late Mrs Edna O'Brien who, whilst at the annual Gilbeys dinner in 1952, was offered a glass of that revered Champagne, 'Dom Perignon', by The Honourable John Gilbey. "No thank-you very much," announced Mrs O'Brien to the astonishment of her fellow diners, "I only drink Barossa Pearl."

I am indebted to the writings of both Len Evans and James Halliday which have provided a continuous source of wine erudition and entertainment during my adult life. The immeasurable contributions of these two men, not only to wine literature but to the Australian Wine industry in general, casts an immense shadow in which all other wine writers can but humbly walk.

*I*nstant wine knowledge

A QUICK DEMYSTIFICATION OF WINE

Wine, to put it simply, is fermented grape juice. It is not the enigma that some would have us believe. The mystique, or confusion, often associated with wine is due to three factors: the wide variety of wine styles and grape varieties on the market, the effects of different soil and climate types, ie. region, on wine grapes, and the ability of wine to change, or develop, with bottle age.

Although an understanding of these factors might interest some readers (they are all covered within this book) most wine knowledge is unnecessary for the enjoyment of wine. Knowing that the ancient Greeks moulded a wine coupe from the breast of Helen of Troy, for example, will not make Retsina taste any better (only a blocked nose can do that).

Useful wine knowledge comes only from tasting and drinking as wide a range of wine as possible and from open-minded wine discussion. The most important wine knowledge you will acquire is the discovery of those wine styles that best suit your taste, and when (season, hour, with what food, etc) you most enjoy drinking them. And the rest? Well, that's what you bought this book for isn't it?

SORTING OUT THE WINE SNOBS

Despite the attempts of several wine writers to dispel the myths of wine elitism, there still exists a substantial element of snobbishness throughout the wine world. Wine snobs are a pretentious lot and attempt to feign superiority over others by espousing the wine trivia they have accumulated over the years. They are most readily recognisable by their habit of judging a wine by its producer, price, or region, before having tasted it.

There's a lot of fun to be had with wine-snobs as they tend be in a rush to acquire the most obscure and useless pieces of wine 'knowledge'. They are therefore quite gullible when addressed in a tone of authority. Nonsense comments such as "It's a good wine, but a touch long on the nose for my liking." will often get agreement from a wine snob. Another trick is to discover a wine that the snob considers; "Just ghastly". Find a bottle of this wine, decant it into an empty bottle with a more fashionable label and serve it up. This will sort most wine-snobs out. Of-course the ultimate defence against a wine snob is to acquire some wine knowledge and with it the confidence to say, "That was great, now how about a real drink," as you reach for the Grappa.

Having wine knowledge does NOT make someone a wine-snob, neither does discussing wine in a public place. If you have a desire to learn more about wine, conversations with like minded people is one of the most effective ways of doing so.

* (This article was inspired by Nick Clarke's wonderful pocket-book; "Bluff your way in Wine")

HOW TO TASTE WINE AS THOUGH YOU WERE AN EXPERT

(Or how to bluff your way through a wine tasting)

The next time you visit a winery's cellar door or go to a wine tasting, follow these steps and even the most experienced wine bibber will take you for an expert.

STEP 1: THE FACE OF THE WINE:

Hold the glass by the stem and base - holding the glass by its vessel is a dead give away that you're a novice. On a practical level, this stops you warming the wine and allows you to examine its 'face' properly. Tilt the glass away from you towards a white background, a blank piece of paper will suffice, and inspect the condition of the wine. Young wines should have a brilliant (bright and lucid) appearance.

There should be no clouding with white wines. A young white wine should shimmer with vitality, and the colour can range from almost clear with greenish tints, through the various shades of yellow (a deeply coloured, young white wine generally indicates barrel aging), through to the golds of late harvest wines. As a white wine ages its vibrancy fades and its colour deepens again through the spectrums of yellow to gold until it finally browns. Browning in white wines is a bad sign unless it's a very old dessert wine.

The purple\red rim of a young red wine is the stamp of youth. With age the colour of red wine is said to become 'brick-red' that is; reddish\brown. Eventually the wine's vibrancy will dull and the rim will start to exhibit a tan colour that will slowly turn to brown with age. Certain styles of red wine, most notably those made from Pinot Noir, can sometimes brown very early in their lives. In these cases the colour is disregarded and in no way detracts from the quality or the aging potential of the wine.

BLUFFERS TIP:

The depth of colour is a good indication of how heavily flavoured a wine is. A dark, opaque red wine will generally be full-bodied and densely flavoured. A lighter colour will indicate a lighter wine. So too, the deeper coloured a white wine is, the richer its flavour will be.

STEP 2: NOSING THE WINE.

Swirl the wine around the walls of the glass to release the various volatiles, then place your nose inside the glass and inhale one of nature's greatest aromas. Although trying to identify the amalgam of different fruit and floral aromas in the 'nose' of a wine can assist with classification, the main aim is to try and ascertain quality. However, don't be too judgmental as many 'noses' can be misleading. The idea is to learn by comparing the various aromas to the flavour in the mouth rather than to dismiss a wine because you don't like the way it smells.

BLUFFERS TIP:
If you can't describe the characteristics of a given wines' aroma, or the wine has a vast variety of scents, then it pays to exclaim that the wine is "Wonderfully complex."

STEP 3:   THE MOST IMPORTANT STEP.

At last we can drink the stuff. Take a small sip of the wine and distribute it with your tongue to all parts of the mouth. This is known as 'chewing' the wine and it helps the taster to make a complete assessment. Another favourite technique of wine tasters is to gently suck air through pursed lips whilst holding the wine in the mouth. The purpose of this is to fully release the aromatics in the mouth enabling all of the wine's characteristics to be revealed. Doing this at a wine tasting will dismiss any doubts of your authenticity as an expert. However, beware, suck too hard and you are likely to take some of the wine down the wrong way causing you to cough violently. This will instantly give the game away. This then is for experienced wine bluffers only.

STEP 4:   SWALLOW OR SPIT?

Wine tasters often spit out a wine and this is the accepted practice at wine tastings. This allows the palate to retain a degree of freshness so that other wines might be accessed accurately. Believe it or not, it is also a way by which wine tasters assess each other. A spit down? And why not? The accuracy and distance of one's spit was always a decent gauge of a school-friend's worth. Why not a fellow taster? Incidentally, if you do spit, make sure you allow a small amount of the wine to trickle down your throat. This will help you fully evaluate the wine especially in establishing if the wine has any bitterness. If you are tasting something delicious, then to hell with bluffing, drink the stuff!

BLUFFERS' TIP:
The best place to practice your spitting is in the shower. Fill your mouth with water, purse your lips and aim for the plug hole. Pretty soon you'll be putting out fires.

STEP 5:   HOW LONG?

After you have swallowed or spat, focus on the wine's "finish". The after-taste that the wine leaves in your mouth is one of the most important quality indicators. The finish in no way should be bitter or unpleasant. The longer the taste lingers the better. The "length" of a wine can also be a good indication of the wines aging potential ie. A long finish (assuming that the lingering flavours are that of sweet fruit as opposed to hard acid, alcohol, or bitterness) bodes well for the wine's future development.

BLUFFERS TIP:
One of the best things you can say, when bluffing your way, is: "Hmm, great length," or "Hmm, finishes a bit short." Comments such as these will have even the most cynical wine-maker racing out the back to open a bottle of the 'good stuff'.

HOW THE WINE TRADE FUNCTIONS

And the value of a good retailer

The Australian wine industry generally works as follows: a wine producer (winery) sells to a wholesaler/distributor, who then sells to retailers, who sell on to the public. Some small wine producers sell all of their wine direct to the public. Some larger producers distribute their own wines to retailers.

It is a commonly held misconception amongst wine bibbers that wine retailers work on a 100% plus margin. In reality, retailers place a mark-up of between 15 and 40 percent on their wines, 10% for packaged beer and around 20% for spirits. This is not a great deal when you consider the substantial financial outlay involved in setting up and running a wine store. Wine attracts a nation wide sale tax of 26% and an additional liquor-license fee of 11% (13% in N.S.W. & A.C.T, 10% in QLD). I give these figures not to encourage bartering by wine buyers but to debunk the myth of high profits associated with the sale of liquor.

As a general rule of thumb, the better known a wine is, the more competitive its pricing will be. The reason for this is that the more "commercial" brands tend to be advertised at discounted prices by larger retailers in an attempt to attract customers. It is common for large retail chains to sell these "loss leaders" at only a few cents above what they paid for them. The theory is that whilst no money is made on the advertised special, people are attracted to the store where they will buy additional products that are not discounted. When a wine is advertised regularly at a discounted price of $4.99, it is difficult for other retailers to sell it at the recommended retail price of $6.99. Customers complain and shop staff are accused of over charging when in fact they are only trying to make the margin that any other retailer would consider their right. The great value attributed to many Australian wines is often due more to price competition amongst wine-stores than anything else.

While competition is always desirable, heavy discounting of a wine is not. There are some producers who go out of their way to ensure that the image of their wine is not devalued in consumers' minds by such activities. Others producers have paid dearly for not doing so.

There is another, more significant, effect of wine discounting and that is the demise of the smaller, more specialised liquor store. As members of the wine buying public, we dictate the type of wine service we receive by choosing where to shop. By shopping at large retail chains that offer discount prices on certain products but whose staff are incapable of giving expert wine service, we encourage the extinction of our finer retailers who spend the time and money to train their staff and stock a range of slower selling, more interesting wines.

It is a fallacy that shopping at retail chains will save you a lot of money. I have conducted my own surveys into this and found that not only do the finer retailers of this country offer a better and more interesting selection than the average chain store, they are often, across the board, similarly priced. Certainly you might save fifty cents here and even a dollar there, purchasing wines from a wine supermarket, but it pays to keep in mind that effective wine service saves time, disappointment and money. That is not to say that every small retailer is capable of giving such service. The truth is that very few are, however these few are worth searching for. Perhaps is was Emile Peynaud, the great French oenologist, who best summed it up when he said; "The wine you drink is the wine you deserve."

Oh, and seeing I am in to bat for good retailers, I may as well admit that no wine book can hope to compete with the service that a good retailer can offer. The countless new wines that spring up each year have an undeniably erosive effect on any given wine guide. Quite simply, a well informed wine retailer is of incalculable value.

DECANTING WINE

There is a great deal of contention, even amongst the most experienced wine bibbers, over whether a young red wine benefits from exposure to the air through decanting or simply pulling the cork and allowing the wine to "breathe" prior to drinking. Some people believe that if a wine needs air to "open up", to show its best, then there is ample air in the glass for it to do so.

My own experiments in this area have shown that some young reds can benefit, sometimes markedly, from decanting, although only when the wine seemed initially closed (ie. was not showing all of its fruit character). In some instances the wine has absolutely blossomed after decanting gaining an extra dimension of fruit richness. However, simply pulling the cork on a bottle of wine and letting it "breathe" is a complete waste of time. Only a tiny portion of the wine comes in contact with the air resulting in little, if any, effect.

Older red wines are in need of decanting to remove the sediment that is the natural result of the aging process and to allow any 'bottle stink' to escape. I have, however, seen many older wines ruined by being allowed to breathe so long after being decanted that the delicate flavours in the wine faded and oxidised characteristics developed. All wine should be served immediately after decanting.

In my experience, there is never any reason to decant a white wine even though some whites may have formed some harmless tartrate crystal sediment, affectionately known as wine diamonds.

HOW TO DECANT AN AGED RED

STEP 1
The wine should be stood up for at least an hour, preferably longer, to allow the sediment to settle at the base of the bottle.

STEP 2
Cut the capsule around the top lip of the bottle. If there is any 'build-up' around the opening then it should be wiped away with a clean, damp cloth.

STEP 3
Remove the cork carefully. If the wine is old take care not to break the cork midway. "Screwpull" corkscrews are the surest bet. Clean any excess cork or residue away.

STEP 4
Light a candle and place it under the bottle of wine. This will enable you to see the 'heart' of sediment, which should settle in the shoulder of the bottle and slowly move towards the neck as you pour the wine. If you don't have a candle then a torch might do, or alternatively, decant over a white surface with a strong light above.

STEP 5
Pour the wine slowly and in a continuous stream, as gently as possible so as not to disturb the sediment, until you have drained almost all of the brilliant wine away from its lees. When the sediment is touching the neck, threatening to pour out with the remaining wine, this is the time to stop decanting. You will generally be left with about 1 inch of wine in the base of the bottle.

* If you are decanting a young wine to simply give it some "air" (as previously discussed) then there is no need for a candle. Simply pour the wine, gently and in a steady stream, into a decanter, leave it for ten minutes and then serve. If you don't have an appropriate serving vessel then use a clean glass jug or vase, rinse out the bottle, and making sure that there isn't any water remaining in the bottle, carefully pour the wine back into it.

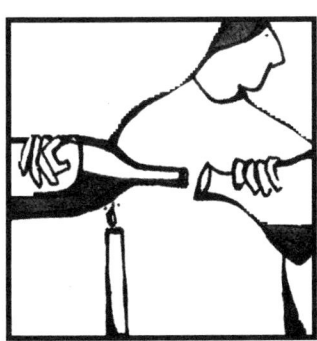

INSTANT WINE KNOWLEDGE

17

A WHINGE ABOUT OUR RESTAURANTS

A great many Australian restaurants, including some of our most respected, show ignorance and\or a lack of interest when it comes to the wine service they offer. This is surprising when one considers the intense competition in the food industry and the emphasis placed on wine by Australian diners. It is a little known fact that Australian's drink more wine per capita than any other English speaking nation and visiting wine makers are often astounded by the high level of wine knowledge amongst members of the general public. Indeed, I have heard it said that Australian wine drinkers are amongst the most erudite in the world. This last assertion is of-course debatable, however, our enthusiasm for wine and wine knowledge is not.

Many restaurateurs seem unaware how many people are turned away from their establishments by poor wine service. No wines by the glass or half bottle for the moderate drinker, exceedingly high mark-ups, poorly constructed wine lists, inappropriate wine glasses and no one capable of giving wine advice or correctly decanting an aged red are constant frictions for the Australian diner. On top of this, many restaurateurs have the gall to refuse B.Y.Os on the basis that they survive on the money they make from liquor. Surely then, it follows that the wine bibber should expect a modicum of service and selection when they dine at such establishments.

When restaurants price their wines, many work on a profit margin of 100% or more, that is, they look at what the wine cost them and effectively double this figure to establish the selling price. Such profit margins are easily justified in establishments that offer complete wine service. I am speaking of restaurants that employ a sommelier or alternatively undertake a program of staff training; restaurants that offer a wide selection of wine, foreign and local, young and mature, and that outlay considerable money on quality glassware. To justify these costs such restaurants may be forced to work on even higher margins, yet many do not. It is baffling however, that many cafes, bistros and restaurants that offer none of these services, feel justified in selling their wines at similar prices.

Many restaurateurs will cite several obstacles that prevent them from offering effective wine service. Let's deal with some of these:

Restaurateur: "If we let one person bring a bottle of wine B.Y.O then we have to let all of our customers."

Diner: Only make the exception for rare or aged bottles of wine or construct a wine list that includes such choices as aged and foreign wines. If someone has a special bottle of wine that they would like bring to dinner, a fair compromise would be to charge a $5-$10 corkage (per bottle).

Restaurateur: "There is always wastage when we serve wines by the glass."

Diner: Machines can be purchased to prevent opened bottles of wine from spoiling for over a week. Alternatively offer a wide selection of half bottles.

Restaurateur: "Good wine glasses are expensive."

Diner: This is often true, however, good examples of I.S.O. tasting glasses, which can be used as multi-purpose glasses as well as being ideal for the appreciation of wine, are currently available for under $4 (wholesale) per glass.

Even such things as staff training can be organised with a minimum of cost. Recently a Sydney cafe owner asked me to construct a wine list for his menu. He claimed that staff turn over was too high to justify any outlay on staff training, so I was contracted to review the wines on the menu and suggest which foods might best compliment them. Much in the same way a sommelier (wine waiter) would have offered such advice verbally, this bistro offered it in a written form on its wine list. New staff were shown how to decant a wine, when it was necessary, and how to serve wine properly. And there you have it, instant wine service at very little cost.

Those who work in the restaurant industry should be the pedagogues of the wine drinking public, challenging our palates with new food and wine combinations. Tragically, many in such positions see themselves, as do their employers, as table servers and little else.

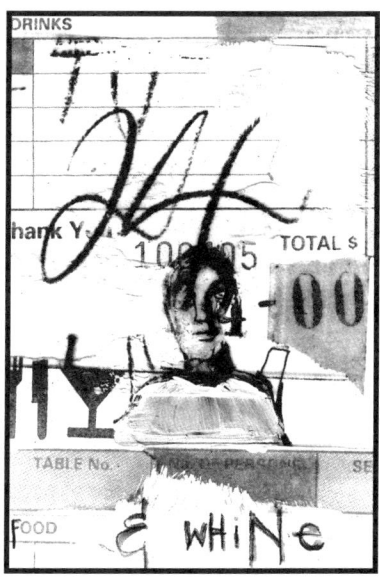

THE AGING OF WINE

One of the most common wine myths is that all wine improves with age. It would be more accurate to say that wine changes with age, sometimes for better, sometimes for worse. Many Australian wines, such as commercial whites and light red styles, are made for immediate consumption and will generally deteriorate with cellaring. Even when a wine has 'cellaring potential', whether or not you should lay it down is a question of personal taste. For example, although many Clare and Eden Valley Rieslings have been drunk with great pleasure at ten or twenty years of age, some prefer the fresh, citrus-like fruitiness of these wines at a young age (1-3 years). It is therefore important to establish what type of flavours you prefer from your wines prior to aging them.

Having said this, a wine cellar can provide a great hobby and, of-course, some very good drinking. What you'll need is a quiet storage place with constant temperature (on the cool side), minimum light, a big padlock on the door, and some cash (the more the better). Many full-flavoured Australian reds, including some under ten dollars, will improve with a certain amount of bottle age. They tend to soften and develop more refined, complex (interesting) flavours with time. Many Australian dry whites (especially over $10) will benefit from at least short term cellaring (1-3 years). Those that will improve with longer periods of cellaring tend to start their lives as tight, restrained wines. By this I mean they exhibit a balance of all their components which gives them a deceptive lightness in the mouth. With age, the colour of white wines deepen and the characteristics of toast, butter and honey evolve along with an added viscosity in the mouth. It is worth keeping in mind that mature wines are typically far better with food than their younger, rough around the edges, counterparts.

It is preferable to buy at least six bottles of the same wine to lay down. This way a wine can be drunk at various stages of development giving the drinker valuable experience, and the ability to check on how the wine is "travelling" without consuming the entire cache. Obviously, with expensive or rare wines, the purchase of such quantities may not be possible. If you only have one or two bottles of a particular wine, you can always consult wine guides, good retailers, or contact the winery for the appropriate drinking time.

When is a wine ready to be drunk? Removing personal taste from the equation, the ideal time to consume a wine is when it shows just enough bottle age complexity, has lost the brashness and simplicity of its youth, yet still retains its freshness. Do not make the mistake of assuming that if a wine drinks well now it is in need of further cellaring. If a wine tastes great today, then what are you waiting for?

When a red wine passes its prime it starts to lose fruit richness and length of flavour. This allows the acid in the wine to dominate the palate and the fruit characters to become more and more concentrated in the front of the mouth. When white wines pass their best, especially in the case of inexpensive wines and many Australian Chardonnays, the richness brought on with age comes to dominate the acidity in the wine causing it to taste 'flabby' or 'fat'. After this stage the wine will start to shed its flavour much in the same way a red wine does. Over aged wines, most commonly whites, can also develop a vanillin, creamy aroma and flavour, that will eventually eclipse the other characters in the wine.

For those not interested in going to all the effort of establishing their own cellar, yet still wanting to try some aged wine, most good wine retailers will offer a selection, although these will often be pricey. For better value, I would suggest contacting one of the wine auctioneers such as Langtons Fine Wines.

Australian wines which tend to benefit from age: Lower Hunter Valley Semillon (unwooded & dry); most full-bodied red wines; Eden Valley, Clare Valley and Mount Barker Rieslings; selected sweet whites, vintage port styles, and Sparkling Burgundy.

OAKY DOKEY? OAK & ITS EFFECT ON WINE

Firstly, to answer the most common question in regard to this subject: "What does oak taste like?" Like oak! Is the obvious answer. Anyone who has smelt a new oak barrel fresh from its plastic wrapping knows what to look for, especially in the aroma of a young, oaked wine. For the wine-taster, vanilla is the most obvious way oak manifests itself in the aroma and flavour of a young wine, and with American oak the flavour imparted tends to be stronger and lean towards the coconut spectrum (sometimes described as 'Malibu'). Cedar is another descriptive often used in an attempt to describe the perfumed, resinous / sap character that oak sometimes gives a wine. Spices, such as nutmeg and cinnamon, are also commonly used descriptives as are 'toasty' or 'smoky', although in white wines these can be bottle-age characteristics. Chocolate is also a characteristic of barrel aging and is most commonly apparent in warm climate reds that have received some American oak treatment.

Winemakers have several options when it comes to their usage of oak. Firstly, there is the choice between American and French oak, (some Eastern or Central European oak is used although this is less common). American oak is prized for its ability to compliment richer red wines, especially Shiraz, and as a less expensive alternative to French oak. French oak is prized for its subtlety which allows it to compliment a wine without dominating its more subtle nuances.

The second choice to be made is how, and for how long, the oak is to be seasoned (pre-aged). Is it to be air dried, or kiln dried? Generally speaking, air dried is preferred and for at least three years although this is expensive. Some wine makers therefore prefer to season the oak staves themselves before sending them to be coopered.

Thirdly, and equally importantly, wine-makers must choose the level of toast that a barrel is given. As part of the barrel making process the staves of oak are supported over a flame so that they can be bent into shape. This literally toasts the inside of the barrel. By raising the temperature of the flame and by extending the period of time the barrel is held over it, the cooperage can offer a winemaker barrels with high, medium or low levels of toast. Lightly toasted barrels tend to impart more overtly woody, oaky flavours to the wine whilst heavier toasts tend to impart characters described as: toasty, smoky, coffee, spicy (nutmeg, cinnamon, five spice). Heavily toasted American oak often imparts a charred character into the wine sometimes manifesting itself as a pleasant charred/smoked meat character.

Finally, there is the option of using oak chips, as opposed to barrels, in the wine making process. Here again there is a variety of toast levels available, with similar flavour consequences. The decision to use oak chips is a purely economic one. They offer the winemaker a less expensive way to impart sweet, vanilla oak flavours to a wine yet they can never fully replicate the beneficial effects of barrel treatment. The oak character they impart tends to be more overt and not as well integrated into the wine's overall flavour and there is also a touch of bitterness that some associate with their usage. Despite these negatives, when used judiciously, oak chips can enhance the flavour of inexpensive commercial wines, where it would be impossible to justify the expense of new oak barrels.

Apart from oak flavour and aroma, a wine is given another dimension by aging and\or fermenting in oak barrels. In red wines, oak treatment tends to soften the wine and give extra tannin (the chalky grip felt in the mouth). Tannin is also derived from grape seeds and skins. Whilst aging in the barrel, wine absorbs tiny quantities of oxygen through the microscopic pores of the oak in a gentle process of oxidisation that gives the wine added complexity, that is, it gives the wine other aromas and flavours that are not derived from the grapes themselves or even from the oak directly. During barrel aging a percentage of the wine's water content evaporates which serves to concentrate the flavour of the wine.

The use of oak in white wines has changed dramatically in Australia over the last five vintages. The richly flavoured, oaky white has almost overnight become a dinosaur to our ever refining palates. White wines labelled as "Classic dry" and "Unwooded", including the ubiquitous "Unwooded Chardonnay", are becoming more and more popular. Winemakers have no doubt realised that by using less new oak (with each usage an oak barrel imparts less flavour, old barrels used many times do not impart any oak flavour), or no oak at all, they can make a hefty saving and also produce wines with a lot more elegance and appeal.

Many fine Australian Chardonnays and red wines do, however, receive a high proportion of new oak treatment. In these cases (ideally speaking) the fruit is of sufficient quality and power to cope with the oak, which, through barrel fermentation and bottle age becomes fully integrated and enhances the wine by adding to its weight, aroma, flavour and aging potential.

Strangely enough, whilst the trend in Australian white wines has moved towards more subtle oak treatment, the drift has been in the opposite direction with our red wines. Many Australian wine-makers have seemingly adopted the catch cry "No wood, no good" and more and more reds, especially young Shiraz wines, are arriving on retailers shelves, oak dominant, with sweet vanilla and coconut aromas and flavours masking the fruit flavours of the wine. Certainly it is true that with time oak character can subside, but so does fruit. As a result, many of these wines will remain overtly oaky until they have passed their prime.

Not all wines that are oak treated (fermented and\or matured in oak) have a dominant oak flavour. In better wines, the oak element is in perfect harmony with the fruit flavours which can make it difficult for the taster to distinguish any obvious oak character. Well handled oak is announced by its subtlety. That is to say, in fine wine, all components are expected to be in balance. Oak is simply another one of these components, its purpose being to add an extra dimension without dominating the whole.

HOW WHITE WINE IS MADE

stalks removed

CRUSHER / DESTEMMER

must is passed through refrigerated tubing to prevent oxidation

HEAT EXCHANGER

AIRBAG PRESS

temperature controlled

STAINLESS STEEL FERMENTATION TANK

maturation in new or used oak perhaps on lees - fermentation may occur in barrel

OAK BARRELS

WINE FILTER

BOTTLE AGEING PRIOR TO RELEASE

HOW RED WINE IS MADE

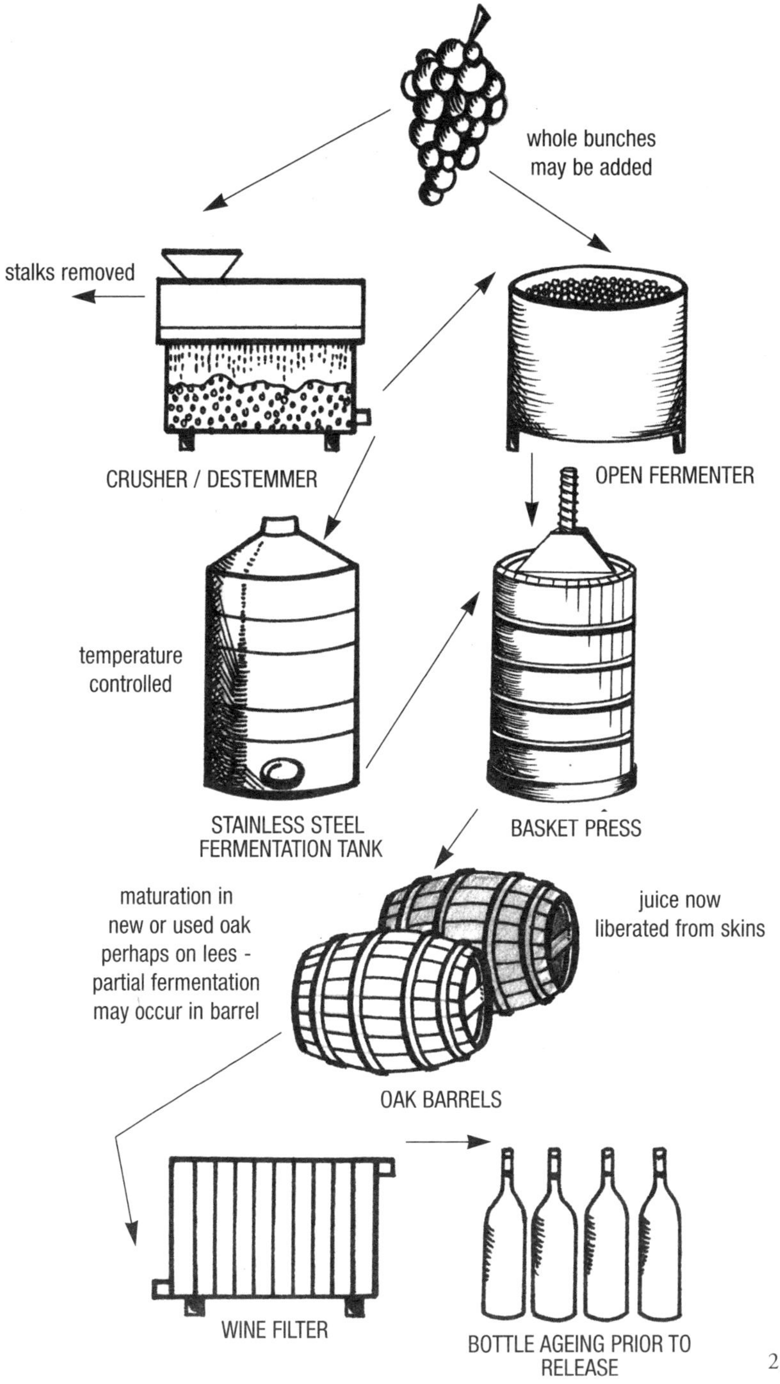

INSTANT WINE KNOWLEDGE

whole bunches may be added

stalks removed

CRUSHER / DESTEMMER

OPEN FERMENTER

temperature controlled

STAINLESS STEEL FERMENTATION TANK

BASKET PRESS

maturation in new or used oak perhaps on lees - partial fermentation may occur in barrel

juice now liberated from skins

OAK BARRELS

WINE FILTER

BOTTLE AGEING PRIOR TO RELEASE

WINE ADDITIVES

The 'preservatives' myth

This is a short glossary of wine 'additives' and techniques of wine enhancement. Each listing contains an explanation as to why these methods are used by wine makers worldwide, as well as an attempt to debunk the mythology that surrounds them.

Sulphur Dioxide: The most maligned of wine additives, sulphur is an extremely effective preservative and disinfectant that has been used in wine making for over 2000 years. It was used by the Romans along with pitch and resin to prepare the barrels and Roman writers such as Cato and Pliny, made mention of its value in the wine-making process. Today Sulphur (principally in the form of Sulphur Dioxide, SO_2) is used by virtually every winemaker, in every country, primarily as a preservative and disinfectant, and to prevent oxidation. SO_2 also inhibits or kills bacteria and wild yeasts that may be present in the wine and encourages a quick, clean fermentation. In the vineyard Sulphur is used to protect vines against both powdery mildew and downy mildew.

Australian labelling law requires that any addition of sulphur dioxide be listed on the wine label either under its own name or as "Preservative (202)". European wine-makers are under no such obligation and hence do not list such additions. Sulphur dioxide usage is however as vital, both in the vineyard and winery, to European winemakers as it is to their Australian counterparts. It is therefore a revelation for many wine retailers to learn, from their more vocal customers, that foreign wines are less likely to give them a hangover because they don't contain any of those "nasty preservatives". The sooner some testing is done into this remarkable phenomena the better.

The question of the potential health danger that SO_2 poses to asthmatics is an interesting one. I am yet to come across any conclusive evidence proving that it is the sulphur in wine that is the problem. There are several other naturally occurring substances in wine, such as acids, phenolics, and alcohol which, by encouraging an increase in ventilation, could equally trigger a reaction in such patients. Still, some doctors insist that it is indeed Sulphur that is the problem. If their conclusions are accurate, and the relatively marginal levels of Sulphur dioxide present in wine can have a negative impact on the health of asthmatics, then many other foodstuffs must be positively lethal. The fact is that sulphur dioxide is widely used, often more liberally, throughout the food and beverage industries, especially in the production of fruit juices and dried fruits. James Halliday and Hugh Johnson have noted in their book; "The Art and Science of Wine", that "relatively few premium quality table wines have total Sulphur Dioxide levels in excess of 100 milligrams per litre. These levels are quite low by overall food standards. Fresh fruit salad and vegetable salad in health food bars frequently contains 200 milligrams per litre of free sulphur dioxide, while other semi-processed foods and beverages contain significantly higher levels."

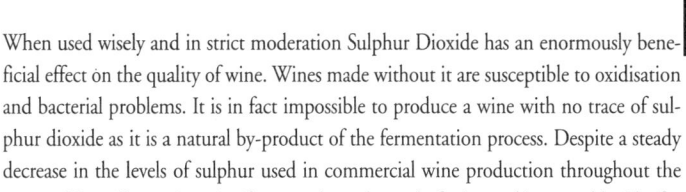

When used wisely and in strict moderation Sulphur Dioxide has an enormously beneficial effect on the quality of wine. Wines made without it are susceptible to oxidisation and bacterial problems. It is in fact impossible to produce a wine with no trace of sulphur dioxide as it is a natural by-product of the fermentation process. Despite a steady decrease in the levels of sulphur used in commercial wine production throughout the 1900s, SO2 will remain a significant and worthy tool of wine making, world wide, for the foreseeable future.

Ascorbic acid: More commonly known as vitamin C, ascorbic acid is naturally present in grapes. It is used in white wine production as it helps to prevent oxidisation. Under Australian labelling laws any addition of vitamin C to a wine is required to be listed as either "Antioxidant (300)" or "Ascorbic acid added" while fruit juices list its usage as "Vitamin C added". Vitamin C is not used in the production of red wines.

Chaptalisation: Often called 'enrichment', chaptalisation involves the addition of sugar to raise a wines alcoholic strength and hence its richness of flavour and body. This addition of extra sugar can come in the form of: grape must, concentrated grape must, rectified concentrated grape must (RCGM) or sugar. Whilst sugar additions are common in Northern Europe (including France), North Eastern regions of USA, throughout Canada, Brazil, Japan, and in much of New Zealand, the practice is illegal in Australia where only concentrated grape must can be used.

Acidification or acid adjustment: The practice of adding additional acid (mostly tartaric although citric and malic are permitted, all these being present in the grape) is widely practiced in Australia. It is used mostly in warmer climates to balance the wine, much in the same way as chaptalisation is used to balance the wines of the world's cooler regions. Acid is best added prior to fermentation. It helps to brighten the colour of the wine and freshen its flavour and aromas. The addition of acid is also permitted in many European wine regions, such as Bordeaux and Burgundy in France, as long as the same wine has not also undergone chaptalisation.

This listing is brief yet largely complete. Wine is a natural product and contains little that is not found in the grape or results from the FERMENTATON process. Winemaking, at its highest level, is an art form whose ultimate aim is to trap the qualities inherant in the grape. Such expressions as "great wine is made in the vineyard" and "a winemaker can only spoil a wine, never improve it" reflect this reality. For these reasons, bottled wine remains one the least tampered with preserved food products on the market.

UNDERSTANDING AUSTRALIAN WINE LABELS

Australian wine producers are not required to list either grape variety or region on their labels and some do not, preferring simply a brand name such as "Virgin Hills" or "Dry Red No 1". They are however required to list the address of the winery. This misleads many wine buyers into assuming that the wine in the bottle came from grapes grown at the address given. Although for the two examples given above this is the case, such an assumption is often incorrect especially in the case of wines in the lower price brackets. Wine labels that do list grape varieties are required by law to list them in order of volume. In other words a Cabernet Merlot will be a wine made from predominantly Cabernet Sauvignon with Merlot being used in lessor quantity. The same rules applies to the use of Regional descriptions.

WITTGENSTEIN'S	winery
YARRA VALLEY	region from which at least 85% of grapes are sourced
CHARDONNAY	grape variety
1994	vintage
71A GRAPEJUICE RD LILLYDALE, VICTORIA 4121	winery address
12.5% 750 ML	alcohol content
PRESERVATIVE 220 ADDED	sulphar dioxide added

Wine regions

WINE BLENDING & THE MEANING OF REGION

Blending is not a dirty word. Many of Australia's great wines are blends in one way or another. Blending wines from different regions or different grape varieties, enables producers to create a consistency of quality that would be otherwise difficult. This flexibility has also created an air of innovation for which our wine makers are famous. It was this creative spirit that led to Max Schubert's creation of Australia's most famous wine, Penfolds Grange (a Shiraz blended from several wine regions sometimes with the inclusion of a small parcel of Cabernet Sauvignon.). Only initiative and experimentation will lead to other great wines being developed in the future and a better understanding of what each region has to offer.

For a number of reasons, the geographical location of a winery can mean little in terms of the wine-styles it produces. Firstly, blending grapes from two or more regions is common practice in Australia and, as I have suggested, wine drinkers are often better off for it. Secondly, regional title (Barossa Valley, Coonawarra etc) on wine labels can be uninformative. Two wineries within the same region will often produce strikingly different wines from the same grape variety simply by the choices they make in the processing of the wine. Differences in the clone and age of the vines, differences in soil type or microclimate, as well as cropping levels, oak treatment, etc, will all affect the quality and style of wine produced. Also, according to the current Australian labelling laws, a wine need only be made from *80% of the grape variety(s) stated on the label and only 80% of the grapes used need to derive from the region listed. Hence a wine labelled 'Coonawarra Cabernet Sauvignon' must be produced from at least 80% Cabernet Sauvignon grapes, and at least 80% of the grapes used in the wine need to have been sourced from within the defined boundary of the Coonawarra region. Therefore, such a wine may in fact be a blend of 60% Coonawarra Cabernet, 20% Coonawarra Shiraz, and 20% McLaren Vale Cabernet and still fulfil its legal requirements. For these reasons, certain wines may exhibit characteristics that have little to do with either the region or the grape variety recorded on the label.

This is not to say that the region of a given wine leaves no imprint. Many wine-makers produce wine from the grapes of one region and in these examples there are often strong similarities in the style of wine produced. Also, certain regions will often show a clear affinity with certain grape varieties and styles of wine. For example some Australian regions produce intensely flavoured Pinot Noir along with crisp & elegant Chardonnay while other regions will produce rich and blowsy Chardonnay, robust, high alcohol Shiraz and weakly flavoured Pinot Noir. For these reasons, it is very handy to have an idea of what each region does best.

* From 1997, as part of Australia's new trade agreement with the EEC, Australian wines must contain 85% (rather than 80%) of the region and grape varieties stated.

AUSTRALIAN WINE REGIONS AND WHAT THEY DO BEST

In this section I have attempted to summarise what each wine area does best. This does not mean that those wine styles which are not listed below each region should be dismissed (there are always exceptions), although it is a signal to tread carefully. In short, this is a listing of the specialities of each region. Coonawarra, for example, is capable of producing some very good Riesling, Sauvignon Blanc, and Chardonnay, however, its reds are clearly the stars of that area and as such it is these that are discussed here. I have not bothered listing every region as ultimately this is a wine-buyers' guide and while many regions play an important part in producing wine grapes, if they are not listed on wine labels, they are of little significance in the choices made by wine buyers.

AUSTRALIA'S WINE REGIONS

VICTORIA

BENDIGO \ HEATHCOTE

This is one of Australia's great red wine regions producing rich, full-bodied wines which can be long lived. The Cabernet Sauvignons can be exceptional as BALGOWNIE and PASSING CLOUDS have shown many times and the Shiraz, especially those from around Heathcote rival the nearby Great Western region.

> **Recommended drinking:** Balgownie, Chateau Le Amon, Hanging Rock (Heathcote Shiraz), Jasper Hill, Mount Ida, Passing Clouds, Water Wheel, amongst others.

GIPPSLAND

One of the many Australian regions with more potential than production. NICHOLSON RIVER VINEYARDS produce powerful Cabernet Sauvignon and Pinot Noir (yes such Pinots do exist) and a magnificent, world class Chardonnay that has the weight and structure to overpower most reds. McALLISTER VINEYARDS make an wonderfully elegant yet rich Cabernet blend and BASS PHILLIP produce some of Australia's finest Pinot Noir. The styles of wine produced by these wineries have little in common, making it impossible to generalise about the region, except to say, that all of these wines are of a very high quality. Production is tiny making the wines of Gippsland painfully difficult to find. Those interested should therefore contact the wineries.

GOULBURN VALLEY

Another region whose wine styles are impossible to generalise about, except to say, with the exception of the subtle Tahbilk Marsanne, they are full of flavour. CHATEAU TAHBILK produce full flavoured, long lived reds and a delicious dry white made from Marsanne. MITCHELTON produce a vast range of wines, often representing tremendous value as their Blackwood Park Riesling demonstrates. TISDALL'S MOUNT HELEN vineyards are capable of producing fine wines especially with Merlot.

GEELONG

A region seemingly well suited to a wide variety of grape varieties. Geelong has a small band of producers making excellent, full flavoured wines. Richly flavoured Pinot Noir, Shiraz, Chardonnay and Cabernet Merlot of the highest quality are made by BANNOCKBURN with the wines of SCOTCHMAN'S HILL excellent also.

> **Recommended drinking:** Bannockburn, Clyde Park, Idyll vineyards, Scotchman's Hill, amongst others.

GRAMPIANS (Great Western)

The Grampians region, with due reverence to the Barossa, McLaren Vale and Heathcote, produces some of the finest, and most interesting Shiraz this country has to offer along with first class Cabernet Sauvignon and some richly flavoured Chardonnay also.

> **Recommended drinking:** Best's Great Western, Cathcart Ridge, Four Sisters (Mount Chalambar), Montara, Mount Langi Ghiran, amongst others.

HEATHCOTE (See Bendigo)

MACEDON
(Sunbury, Romsey, Macedon Ranges, Mount Macedon, Lancefield, Kyneton)

Wines from this region are mostly labelled according to their sub region (listed above). As the length of this list suggests, the Macedon region is a wide area of land encompassing many different soil types and microclimates. A common theme which runs throughout these areas, to various degrees, is an extremely cool and windy climate. Local winemakers, desperate to get their fruit ripened, have been known to make secret sacrifices to appease the weather gods. In the years when such ceremonies work, surprisingly more often than not, the wines produced are of the highest quality.

Continued over...

Recommended drinking: Craiglee (produces one of Australia's finest Shiraz amongst other wines), Goonawarra (delicious Semillon and Cabernet Franc), Knights Granite Hills, Virgin Hills (A fine single-vineyard red) The sparkling wines produced by Cope Williams (labelled as "Romsey"), Cleveland Estate and Hanging Rock (labelled as "Macedon"), are some of Australia's finest.

MORNINGTON PENINSULA

A high quality area especially for Chardonnay, Pinot Noir and medium bodied Cabernet Sauvignon.

Recommended drinking: Dromana Estate, Elgee Park, Main Ridge Estate, Merricks Estate, Moorooduc Estate, Stoniers, T'Gallant, amongst others.

RUTHERGLEN

It's been said many times but it seems that few people are listening. The Muscat and Tokays (soon to undergo a name change) of the Rutherglen area are amongst the finest and certainly the most underpriced dessert\after dinner wines in the world. It looks like it's going to take an off shore explosion in demand for these wines, and the subsequent price rises that we are now witnessing with our table wines, before Australians truly appreciate how magnificent these wines are. Rich, tannic (mouth drying), high alcohol, "knife & fork" reds are typical of the region ranging from heavyweights, Shiraz, Cabernet, and blends, to the monolithic Durif reds.

Recommended drinking: All Saints, Baileys, Bullers, Campbells, Morris, Rosewood, Stanton & Killeen, amongst others.

PYRENEES (Redbank, Avoca, Moonambel)

This region produces full bodied red wines of outstanding quality along with some excellent, full flavoured Chardonnay and good value sparkling wines.

Recommended drinking: Chateau Remy, Dalwhinnie, Mount Avoca, Redbank, Taltarni, Warremang, amongst others.

YARRA VALLEY

One of the finest regions for Chardonnay and indisputably the finest for Pinot Noir in the country. Also a tremendous region for Cabernet Sauvignon, and Shiraz seems under utilised if the quality of the YARRA YERING (Dry red No2) and SEVILLE ESTATE wines are anything to go by.

Recommended drinking: Coldstream Hills, Diamond Valley, DeBortoli (Yarra Valley), Gembrook Hill, Lillydale Vineyards, Long Gully, Mount Mary, Oakridge, Seville Estate, St Huberts, Tarrawarra, Yarra Ridge, Yarra Yering, Yering Station, Yerringberg, amongst others.

NEW SOUTH WALES

LOWER HUNTER VALLEY

The lower Hunter's unwooded **Semillons** are not only unique in style but amongst the greatest Australian dry white wines. These wines begin their lives as soft, dry, austerely flavoured whites that will develop, given time in the bottle, into rich full flavoured wines, often described as "toasty" and "honeyed". Some great examples are able to retain an incredible freshness and elegance for many years. Many outstanding **Chardonnays** are also produced much to the surprise of those who consider Chardonnay to be a cool-climate grape.

The Lower Hunter makes a style of Shiraz that is often soft and medium bodied, with the primary flavours of plums and spice often intermingled with earth, aniseed, and leather characters. It is these last three rustic characteristics, along with the velvety smoothness that these wines develop with age, that make Hunter Shiraz such a distinctive wine which many people enjoy, while others, preferring the mid-palate richness of Shiraz grown further South, can find unappealing. You be your own judge. These wines can be extremely long lived and like the Semillons of this region, often need time in the bottle to show their best. Better examples can be amongst our most complex red wines.

Recommended Semillon producers: Allanmere, Briar Ridge, Brokenwood, Lindemans, McWilliams, Petersons, Rothbury Estate, Tyrrells, amongst others.

Recommended Chardonnay producers: Allanmere, Brokenwood, Lakes' Folly, Lindemans, Petersons, Pooles Rock, Tyrrells, amongst others.

Recommended Shiraz producers: Briar Ridge, Brokenwood (Graveyard), Lindemans, McWilliams (Individual Vineyard & O'Shea releases), Petersons, Rothbury Estate, Saddlers Creek, Tyrrells, amongst others.

UPPER HUNTER

This region, situated further north than the lower Hunter, can produce markedly different whites to its sister region. The Semillons are generally oak treated giving the wines more richness in their youth and the flavours of buttered toast and vanilla. The Chardonnays are often broader in flavour and again show generous oak influence. Reynolds, produce a more traditional Semillon in the ilk of the lower Hunter.

Recommended producers: Horseshoe Vineyards, Reynolds, Rosemount, amongst others.

MUDGEE

West of the Hunter and North West of Sydney, the Mudgee region is known mostly for its reds, the best generally being made from Cabernet Sauvignons and Cabernet blends. These wines can be deeply coloured and flavoured and, in such cases, will often repay medium term cellaring (3-8 years).

Recommended producers: Augustine, Botobolar, Craigmoor, Huntington Estate, Montrose, Rothbury (when labelled as Mudgee), Seldom Seen, Thistle Hill, amongst others.

CANBERRA

A region still in the early stages of development made up of small to tiny wine producers. It is still uncertain which varieties will emerge as best suited to the hot-cold climate of Canberra, but some very fine reds and whites have been produced by Lark Hill and Doonkuna Estate amongst others.

Other Recommended producers: Clonakilla, Jeir Creek, Madew, Amongst others.

GRIFFITH/ RIVERINA

An area that was originally put on the fine-wine map by one producer and one wine: DE BORTOLI'S "Noble One" Botrytis Semillon. The first vintage of this luscious dessert wine (1982) went on to become one of the most decorated wines in Australian Show history winning 11 trophies and 45 gold medals. Although it was suggested at the time that this may have been a one-off, freak wine, De Bortoli has subsequently repeated the exercise many times over and now other producers have also stepped in to prove that this region is ideally suited to the production of these unctuous styles. Riverina Botrytis Semillon is typically a powerful wine, searingly rich and sweet, often exhibiting the flavours of apricot nectar, spice, orange-peel, and a whisper of vanillin oak in the better examples. With age these wines will typically evolve honey and toffee overtones.

Continued over...

GRIFFITH

Hot and dry, Griffith is also an efficient producer of bulk and inexpensive dry bottled wines.

Recommended producers of botrytis Semillon: Cranswick Estate, De Bortoli, McWilliams, Miranda, Wilton Estate, Yarra Ridge, Yering Station, amongst others.

SOUTH AUSTRALIA

ADELAIDE HILLS (Including Lenswood, Piccadilly)
See also Eden Valley.

This is a young and exciting area that in recent years has shown stunning results with a wide variety of styles most notably: Pinot Noir, Sauvignon Blanc, and Chardonnay. The theme running through the Pinot Noir is depth of flavour with elegance. Vignerons have been able to produce rich, ripe wines, deeply coloured and flavoured, and with alcohol levels pushing 14%. Yet for all this power, the wines show excellent acidity and a deceptive delicacy in the mouth. Full flavoured, rich Chardonnays are typical of Lenswood with more restrained styles coming from the Piccadilly region. The Sauvignon Blanc produced around Lenswood, as Lenswood Vineyards and Stafford Ridge have shown, can be amongst the finest in Australia.

Recommended producers: Ashton Hills, Grosset ("Piccadilly" Chardonnay & Pinot Noir), Henschke (under their grey Lenswood label), Lenswood Vineyard, Petaluma (Chardonnay), Pibbin, Stafford Ridge, amongst others.

BAROSSA VALLEY

The reds of the Barossa are legendary. Shiraz is the outstanding grape here although many wonderful Cabernet Sauvignons are also produced. At their best these reds are full bodied, richly flavoured and often long lived. Plantings of Grenache, once used primarily in fortified production, are now being used to make dry reds of distinction. Full bodied, oaked Semillon, which is a great alternative for Chardonnay drinkers, is a specialty of the Barossa. Many of Australia's finest "Sparkling Reds" wines also come out of the Barossa.

Recommended producers: Basedows, Charles Cimicky, Charles Melton, E & E, Elderton, Grant Burge, Heritage, Peter Lehmann, Rockford, Turkey Flat, amongst others.

CLARE VALLEY (Watervale, Polish Valley/Polish Hill River, Sevenhill)

Along with the Eden Valley, this region produces Australia's finest Rieslings. These wines are full flavoured and fruity (in the sense that they exhibit loads of fruit character), yet they are generally dry and in some cases bone dry. Clare Rieslings are delicious when drunk young and fresh yet they will in many cases benefit from 5-10 years of bottle age. Great examples are capable of living for decades yet it is a matter of personal taste as to whether they are worth keeping for that long.

The better reds of the Clare are richly flavoured, powerful wines that none the less exhibit a softness, and therefore a certain elegance, in the mouth. The long lived wines of Wendouree are a case in point. These wines are monstrous in terms of weight of flavour and tannin, yet they do not show any of the porty, jammy characters that one associates with wines of similar dimensions. Some makers do aim to achieve, lighter, more restrained reds, however these are not typical of the region.

Recommended producers: Grosset, Jim Barry, Leasingham Domaine, Leo Buring (When labelled as Clare origin), Mitchell, Mount Horrocks, Pauletts, Penfolds Clare Estate, Penwortham, Petaluma (Riesling), Pikes, Sevenhill, Skillogalee, Tim Adams, Tim Knappstein, Wendouree, amongst others.

COONAWARRA

Hailed by many as Australia's greatest red wine region, Coonawarra consistently produces outstanding Cabernet Sauvignons and very fine Shiraz. These reds tend to be richly flavoured, full bodied, and long lived. Price is often a reasonable guideline to quality in this area with a great deal of good value about for the observant bibber.

Recommended producers: Bowen Estate, Brands Laira, Hollick, Katnook Estate, Leconfield, Mildara, Orlando (Jackaranda Ridge, St Hugo), Lindemans (St George, Limestone Ridge, Pyrus), Parker, Penfolds (bin 128 and when labelled), Penley Estate, Petaluma, Estate, Rosemount (Show Reserve Cabernet Sauvignon), Wynns Coonawarra Estate, Zema, amongst others.

EDEN VALLEY

This region has been traditionally included as a sub region of the Barossa or, more recently, as part of the Adelaide Hills. It is my feeling that the Eden Valley region produces wines that are significantly different to either area and therefore deserves a separate listing. I am also of the opinion that regional definition is a problem for wine producers, and the relevant authorities, not for wine writers. Hence I have dealt with the region as it is mostly dealt with on wine labels- independently.

Continued over...

EDEN VALLEY

The Eden Valley produces, along with Clare, many of the finest Rieslings made in this country. These wines typically commence life as elegant citrussy, dry whites, with firm, steely acid. With time they slowly develop into magnificent full flavoured whites with lime and toast flavours, along with the expected aged Riesling characters (discussed under "Riesling" on Pg 143). These wines tend to be less overtly fruity than their Clare counterparts and will often develop more slowly.

Good examples will live and continue improving for a long time, although most will show their best between 5 & 10 years of age. Full bodied yet elegant reds of the highest quality are produced here along with some outstanding Chardonnay.

Recommended producers: Craneford, Henschke, Irvine, Leo Buring (only when labelled as Eden Valley), Mountadam, Orlando (Flaxmans & St Helga), Yalumba (Heggies and Pewsey Vale), amongst others.

MCLAREN VALE (Southern Vales)

A region probably most renown for its traditionally styled, richly flavoured and long lived Shiraz, McLaren Vale now has a deservedly equal reputation for full bodied Cabernet Sauvignon and richly flavoured Chardonnay. Wine styles vary considerably, yet the Shiraz wines are consistently rich and voluptuous, with spice, plum, and chocolate flavours.

Recommended producers: Chapel Hill, Chateau Reynella, Coriole, Hugo, Ingoldby, Maglieri, Seaview, Temple Bruer, Wirra Wirra, Woodstock, Rosemount (Balmoral and when labelled), amongst others.

PADTHAWAY

"Sister" region of Coonawarra noted for its white wines, especially Chardonnay, Sauvignon Blanc and Riesling, along with some soft and flavoursome reds.

Recommended producers: Browns, Hardys (Siegersdorf Riesling and other wines when labelled as Padthaway), Lindemans, Orlando (St Hilary Chardonnay, Lawson's Shiraz), Padthaway Estate, amongst others.

WESTERN AUSTRALIA

LOWER GREAT SOUTHERN REGION (Frankland, Mount Barker, Albany, Pemberton, Manjimup, Denmark and surrounds)

A large, sparsely planted area of land, the Lower Great Southern contains a growing number of sub-regions. The largest selection of wines come from the Mount Barker area where fine, elegant Cabernet Sauvignon, Shiraz and Chardonnay are produced. The dry Rieslings of Mount Barker are truly wonderful. They are typically crisp and zesty dry whites which in their youth are packed with lime, passionfruit, and sometimes, grapefruit flavours. The Cabernets here show none of the grassiness evident in the wines of some other cool-climate regions. Albany appears to be an area for very fine Pinot Noir and Chardonnay if the wines of Wignalls are anything to go by, whilst the Frankland River area produces many fine wines in a variety of styles. Although it is early days yet, Pemberton-Manjimup is already being lauded as the next WA region for super-premium Pinot Noir, Chardonnay and Cabernet Sauvignon wines. In summary, the Lower Great Southern produces restrained, yet supple and full flavoured wines of the highest quality.

Recommended producers: Alkoomi, Forest Hill, Frankland Estate, Goundrey, Houghtons (Frankland River Label), Howard Park, Plantagenet, Salitage, Smithbrook, Wignalls, amongst others.

MARGARET RIVER

A region producing an array of world class wines. Rich yet elegant Chardonnay, full bodied, long lived Cabernet Sauvignon, underappreciated, smooth as velvet Shiraz, crisp and zesty "Classic Dry Whites", along with some very fine Semillons.

Recommended producers: Cape Clairault, Cape Mentelle, Cullen, Evans and Tate, Fermoy Estate, Happs, Leeuwin Estate, Moss Wood, Pierro, Sandstone, Vasse Felix, amongst others.

TASMANIA

Considering the cool, if not cold, climate of Tasmania, it is not surprising that many of the state's best wines have come from the Burgundian grape varieties; Chardonnay and Pinot Noir. The French wine region of Burgundy is also very cool and frequent comparisons have been drawn between its climate and that of Tasmania. Tasmanian producers have also produced fine wines from the Alsatian\German grape varieties of Riesling and Gewurztraminer. Some critics have even gone as far as to say that Riesling has so far produced the finest whites from Tasmania.

Tasmania's wine styles vary considerably yet the whites tend to be crisp and elegant. The better Chardonnays can develop beautifully with age and the Rieslings are full of lime, passionfruit, and herbal flavours. Tasmania has produced some fine Cabernets yet this is a dangerous area for the wine buyer as many thin and vegetal examples exist and even the finer producers struggle with consistency. Seek advice from a good retailer. Fine sparkling wines are produced by Heemskerk (Janz) and Taltarni (Clover Hill).

Recommended producers: Freycinet, Heemskerk, Moorilla Estate, Pipers Brook, Rochecombe, Springvale, amongst others.

Grape varieties and other wine titles

GRAPE VARIETIES AND OTHER WINE TITLES

This listing does not include all the grape varieties grown in Australia. I have set the qualification at varieties which have an important role in the production of quality table and fortified wines and/or varieties that are visible on wine labels. I have been forced to include in this listing, the names of certain French wine styles which are shamelessly used by our wine marketeers. The use of these French Regional titles, such as Chablis, Burgundy, Hermitage, Champagne, Beaujolais, Sauternes, etc, to label Australian wines is a travesty that both highlights the price one pays for relatively unrestricted wine labelling, and the lack of imagination amongst those responsible for marketing our wines.

The often-used argument that this situation has somehow been forced upon producers by a confused market place is laughable. As it stands, Australian wines labelled "White Burgundy" are made in different states from different grape varieties with varying degrees of oak treatment. Nothing but more bewilderment has been created by this labelling. Thankfully, this practice is being phased out by 1997 as part of a trade agreement between Australia and the E.E.C.

WHITE WINES

Auslese

A German term denoting a sweet late harvest wine. Sweeter than spatlese. The grape variety used is often mentioned in the title.

Blanquette

See Clairette

Beerenauslese

A German term denoting a extremely sweet late harvest wine. Sweeter than Auslese.

Botrytis

Botrytis cinerea, also known as noble rot, is a fungus that attacks ripe grape bunches especially in warm, humid conditions. Although feared by producers of dry wines, it is often encouraged by producers of late harvest, dessert styles. In such cases the mould assists the winemaker by helping to shrivel the berries, concentrate the sugar and flavour components of the grape while lending a spicy, orange peel character to the finished wine. Noble rot can also add a zestiness to dry white wines however it is totally detracting in red wines.

Brown Muscat

See Muscat a petit grains

Chardonnay

A white grape which produces a wide array of differing wine styles in Australia, from full bodied, heavily oaked wines, to more restrained (subtly flavoured) styles, through to unwooded, dry styles.

Chasselas

This white grape is the principal variety of Switzerland. In Australia, the small plantings are mostly grown in the Great Western region of Victoria where it is used in the production of sparkling wine and some still wine production. Montara make a pleasant dry wine from this variety.

WHITE WINES

Chenin Blanc

A white grape originating from the Loire Valley of France where it is made into the great white wines of Vouvray and Anjou. In Australia these heights have not been reached and Chenins tend to be soft fruity wines quite often on the sweetish side. The Swan Valley is the exception to this where a rich dry style is produced. This variety lends itself well to blending as is seen in the wonderfully underpriced Houghtons' White Burgundy and some of WA's Classic Dry Whites.

Clairette

A white grape grown mostly in the Hunter Valley where it is sometimes called Blanquette.

Classic Dry White

Who knows? Generally used by Western Australian producers to indicate a zesty dry white blended from Semillon, Sauvignon blanc and sometimes a small quantity of Chardonnay grapes yet without any restrictions on the title; I repeat, who knows?

Colombard

A white grape used to make many white wines and yet rarely given any credit on the wine label. Such wines, in the past, have generally been labelled as "Chablis" or some other French regional title. Colombard is valued for its ability to retain good acid levels in hot climates. In France it is used as one of the grapes from which Armagnac and Cognac are made.

Recommended producers: Primo Estate, amongst others.

Crouchen

A white grape variety which often makes serviceable though, to the best of my knowledge, never great, wines.

Doradillo

A white grape used principally for distillation into sherries and brandy.

WHITE WINES

Frontignac

See "Muscat Blanc a petit grains"

Gewurztraminer

See Traminer

Marsanne

This white grape variety comes from the Rhone Valley in France. In Australia it is mostly grown in the Goulburn Valley of Victoria where it makes a light, crisp white when young and unwooded, that develops with age into a richer, honeyed wine.

Recommended producers: Chateau Tahbilk, Mitchelton (generously oaked adding toasty, resinous characters to the wine), Yeringberg (blended with Rousanne), amongst others.

Muscadelle (Tokay)

White grape used to made the unique Tokay; a fortified wine of Victoria's North East. Less rich than the area's Muscats, the Tokay is still very sweet with wonderful 'toffee' and 'cold tea' flavours. It is one of Australia's greatest, yet least known wines. (See Tokays & Muscats pg186)

Muscat

See Muscat Gordo Blanco or Muscat â petit grains

Muscat of Alexandria

Another name for Muscat Gordo Blanco.

Muscat Blanc â petit grains, Frontignac, Brown Muscat

Although it is used to make fruity, slightly sweet white wines, Frontignac's claim to fame is built on the fortified Muscats of North Eastern Victoria. These are viscous and richly flavoured dessert wines which like the Tokays of the same region are unique to Australia and of the highest possible quality. Yet for all this, these wines remain terribly underrated and as a result there exists a great deal of value in the market place.

WHITE WINES

Muscat Gordo Blanco

Also called Muscat of Alexandria. A white grape that is mostly used for cask wine. In bottled wine it makes, when dry, a spicy white, although mostly used to produce a sweeter, late harvest wine once commonly labelled as Lexia or Spatlese Lexia. Brown Brothers make an excellent dry white from this variety labelled "Dry Muscat Blanc".

Ondenc

Grown mostly in the Grampians (formerly Great Western) region of Victoria where it is used in the production of sparkling wines. Montara make a delicious dry white from this variety.

Palomino

A white grape from Spain which in Australia is generally used, alongside its look-alike Pedro Ximinez, in the production of fortified wines especially sherry.

Pedro Ximinez

A white grape, originally from Spain used to produce bulk wines or fortifieds, mostly sherry. See also Palomino. Campbells make an interesting dry white from this variety.

(Rhine) Riesling

Correctly known simply as Riesling. The 'Rhine' in the title was originally used to differentiate this wine, made from the Riesling grape, from other incorrectly named Rieslings such as "Hunter River Riesling" (actually Semillon) and "Clare Riesling" (once used as a title for Clare Valley Crouchen). The best regions for this grape variety are the Eden valley and the Clare Valley although exceptions abound, most notably Mount Barker and Tasmania. These wines typically start their lives full of citrus, lemon\lime flavours and develop viscosity and toasty aromas with age. Another bottle aged character that develops in these wines is often described by wine tasters as "kerosene". Although this is intended as a complimentary descriptive, I believe it to be an unhelpful one as for many it calls to mind an unpleasant harshness which has nothing to do with these wines. The term I like to use is "aged Riesling character" or simply A.R.C. to designate the viscous, lime/toast characteristics these wine take on with age. Riesling is also used to produce sweet, botrytised whites of great distinction. (See Sweet & Sticky; The Dessert Wines Pg 179)

WHITE WINES

Sauvignon Blanc

A grape variety typically used to produce a pungent style of dry white wine, although some is used in the production of sweet wines and even fortifieds. The intense "grassy" character of some of these wines, sometimes labelled as "asparagus", "green pea" or even "cat's urine" by tasters, makes this a love or hate variety. The best Australian examples have tended to come from the Adelaide Hills, Yarra Valley, Coonawarra and McLaren Vale. Quite commonly blended with Semillon, most notably in Western Australia where the finest examples of this style are produced and often labelled as "Classic Dry White". (See "The Aromatics" on pg 151)

Semillon

A white grape which is unquestionably at its best in the Lower Hunter Valley of N.S.W where it is made into a dry white wine, traditionally unoaked, although not the rule anymore. The traditional style tends to be crisp and light in its youth, developing more toasty richness with time, and good examples can live for decades. The Upper Hunter region of N.S.W also does fairly well with Semillon although these wines tend to be oak treated adding toasty, vanillin flavours and aromas to the wine. The Barossa Valley, along with other South Australian regions, produces a similarly rich style with ripe fruit and toasty oak. The Margaret River region produces striking wines from this variety often with a herbaceous streak and only a whisper of oak. Semillon also lends itself well to the making of dessert wines especially from the Griffith region of NSW

Spatlese

A German term which denotes a late-harvest, riper style of wine. It not necessarily sweet, but in Australia it is nearly always so. It is not as sweet as auslese.

Sylvaner

A white grape which produces a bland wine used mostly for blending. Of minimal importance.

Tokay

See Muscadelle.

WHITE WINES

Traminer or Gewurztraminer

In Alsace, France, this grape variety produces some of the finest and most powerful dry and sweet white wines of the world. In Australia it has never reached these heights and has been mostly blended with Riesling (this concoction labelled Traminer Riesling) to produce unexciting though pleasant whites generally with more than a touch of sugar sweetness. Orlando has, in the distant past, produced some stunning dessert and dry wine styles from this variety, again often blending it with Riesling. Dry whites made from this aromatic grape can be excellent and are ideal with Asian or spicy foods.

Recommended producers: Delatite, Henschke, Lillydale Vineyards, Moorilla, Orlando Flaxman's, Pipers Brook, Tim Knappstein, amongst others.

Traminer Riesling

A blend of Traminer and Riesling.

Trebbiano

A white grape generally used to make cask wine or cheap sparkling. Lends itself well to distillation due to its neutral flavour.

Verdelho

Made famous by its use in Portuguese Madeira. In Australia it is used to produce pleasant, citrussy whites, generally dry but sometimes with a hint of sweetness. Not enough is grown to have a clear concept of regional preference although the Swan Valley in WA and the Hunter in NSW have so far produced the best examples.

Recommended producers: Ashbrook, Houghtons, Pendarves Estate, Moondah Brook, Rothbury, Wyndham Estate, amongst others.

Unwooded Chardonnay

The latest, rather bizarre, twist in the evolution of Australian Chardonnay. These are soft, full flavoured whites that show far more body and overt fruit richness than one might expect from unwooded whites. The exception is the crisp and dry Plantagenet Omrah Chardonnay. Unwooded Chardonnays are best drunk young.

Recommended producers: Chapel Hill, Plantagenet, T'Gallant, Tyrrell's She Oak, amongst others.

RED WINES

Cabernet Franc

A red Grape which makes similarly flavoured, although lighter and softer, wines to Cabernet Sauvignon. It often exhibits a herbal, leafy characteristic that is similar to those found in unripe Cabernet Sauvignon. Generally used for blending with Cabernet Sauvignon although some straight varietal wines are made, most notably by Goonawarra Winery in the Macedon Region, and Tim Knappstein.

Cabernet Merlot

A blended wine made from Cabernet Sauvignon and Merlot grapes.

Cabernet Sauvignon

A red grape that adapts well to wide range of regions, of which Coonawarra in S.A, is the king in Australia. Other regions in which it excels are the Lower Great Southern and Margaret River regions of W.A, The Barossa in S.A, McLaren Vale in S.A, the Yarra Valley along with just about all the other Victorian regions. No areas are to be excluded through snobbery. Cabernet typically produces full bodied wines which can be long lived. It sometimes exhibits a grassy, green capsicum streak, like that seen in Sauvignon Blanc, when grown in the cooler climes. Victorian examples often show a menthol streak often described as mint or eucalyptus. Primary flavour characteristics: Blackcurrant (Ribena, cassis), tobacco (cigar box).

Cinsault

A red grape which produces a softer style of red wine that was formerly labelled as Blue Imperial(Nth Eastern, Vic) and Black Prince(Grampians, Vic). Still used in blended reds, both Cabernet and Shiraz based.

Durif

A red grape grown in North East Victoria and traditionally used in Port production. Also used in this region to produce a red wine which is enormous in every sense of the word and very long lived. North Eastern Victorian Durif is typically highly tannic, deeply coloured, and not for those with a weak heart.

RED WINES

Gamay

The red grape of the Beaujolais region in France. Hardly grown in Australia although a delicious, medium bodied, red is produced from gamay by Sorrenburg winery in Beechworth.

Grenache

Once used primarily in Australia to produce port and bulk wine, Grenache is more and more being used to produce high quality reds wines especially in the Barossa and McLaren Vale regions of South Australia. These wines are typically soft yet full flavoured with a high alcohol content that adds a roundness and a delicious 'sweetness' to the wine.

> **Recommended producers:** Charles Melton "Nine Popes" (A Shiraz-Grenache blend), Clarendon Hills, Crabtree, Ingoldby, Mitchell, Mitchelton III and Penfolds Old Vine (both blended with Shiraz and Mourvedre), Rockford, Temple Bruer, Turkey Flats, amongst others.

Hermitage

A region in France which produces a full bodied and long lived red wine from the Shiraz grape. Used, in the past, on Australian wine labels generally to signify a wine made from Shiraz. Needless to say Australian wine has long since outgrown the need for such copy-cat labelling which is, and always has been, a classic case of cultural cringe.

Malbec

A red grape capable of producing deeply colored and flavoured wine, although it is generally at its best when blended with Cabernet or Shiraz. In these cases it tends to add richness and softness to the blend. Wendouree have made straight varietal wines from this grape, Brian Croser's Sharefarmers Blend is predominantly Malbec, and Taltarni makes a Rose style that is 100% Malbec.

Mataro

A synonym for Mourvedre.

RED WINES

Merlot

A red grape, mostly blended with Cabernet Sauvignon (hence the labelling: "Cabernet Merlot") which tends to soften and 'flesh out' the more austere Cabernet wine. Merlot is also used to make exceptional straight varietal wines which, although being round in flavour can be quite restrained and well structured.

Recommended producers: Clarendon Hills, Evans & Tate, Happs, Irvines, Petaluma, Rosemount, amongst others.

Mondeuse

A red grape variety rarely seen in Australia. Mostly blended with either Cabernet Sauvignon or Shiraz.

Mourvedre (Often called Mataro)

Produces a red wine useful for blending, most notably at Wendouree where it is blended with Shiraz. Mourvedre's thick skinned berries produce wines of good colour and flavour however it can be very tannic on its own. It is one of the most important grape varieties in Spain. Mourvedre has been unpopular amongst Australian winemakers until recently when it has steadily gained flavour as a blending partner for Shiraz and Grenache.

Recommended producers: Penfolds Old Vine, Mitchelton III (both blends including Shiraz and Grenache), Wendouree Shiraz Mataro, amongst others.

Pinot Meunier

The third grape of French Champagne; the small plantings of Pinot Meunier in Australia are also generally used in the production of sparkling wines, although Bests of Great western have made some fine dry reds with this variety.

Pinot Noir

At its best, this grape produces velvet smooth reds with strawberry/cherry fruit often interfused with forest floor/ herbal/ sappy complexity and the zesty acidity that makes them wonderful food wines. They are generally elegant, middle weight reds although there are exceptions such as those produced by Nicholson River and Montara. The best examples tend to come from the cooler climates such as the: Yarra Valley, Mornington Peninsula, Geelong, Lenswood, Gippsland, Lower Great Southern amongst others.

RED WINES

Shiraz

Australia's most widely planted red grape, Shiraz is capable of producing richly flavoured red wines of the highest quality and adapting well to many different regions. The major grape of the Rhone Valley in France where it is called "Syrah".

Sparkling Red/Sparkling Shiraz

A uniquely Australian style of wine, the best examples of Sparkling Shiraz are richly flavoured and soft with a delicate sweetness. They can be very long lived and are traditionally drunk on Christmas day. (See "Sparkling Wines" Pg 189)

Tarrango

A hybrid red grape developed by the CSIRO from a cross between Touriga and Sultana. Can be made into a delicious light red as demonstrated by Brown Brothers.

Zinfandel

A red grape variety from which it is possible to make a wide variety of wines as is the case in California U.S.A where it is made into cask wines, full bodied reds of extremely high quality and pinky coloured wines. In Australia, this variety is mostly grown in WA where Cape Mentelle produce an outstanding, deeply flavoured example. Watch out for future releases by Thistle Hill.

FRENCH REGIONAL TITLES USED ON AUSTRALIAN WINES

Beaujolais

A region in France producing light to medium bodied wines made from the Gamay grape.

Bordeaux & Bordeaux Blanc

One of the greatest of French wine regions, Bordeaux is best known for its production of outstanding red wines from the Cabernet Sauvignon, Merlot, Cabernet Franc, and Petit Verdot grape varieties, as well as earthy dry whites made from Sauvignon Blanc and Semillon. This title is, thankfully, rarely used on Australian wine labels anymore.

Burgundy & White Burgundy

Again a region of France, Burgundy makes its best red wine from the Pinot Noir grape and its white wines from Chardonnay. Ironically, Australian wines that have carried these titles were rarely, if ever, made from these grape varieties, and had nothing in common with their French counterparts in terms of style.

Chablis

A French region noted for its crisp, flinty Chardonnays. Unfortunately the labelling of cheap Australian whites (never Chardonnays) as Chablis has destroyed its reputation in this country. Chablis has also been used as a title for Hunter Valley Semillon and many great examples of this wine were labelled as such.

Champagne

A French region famous for its sparkling wines; not to be confused with "Methode Champenoise" which indicates that the wine has been made according to the guidelines set down for French Champagne production. In the past this term has been incorrectly used on Australian sparkling wines.

Sauternes

One of the great sweet wines, along with Barsac, of the Bordeaux region in France. Has been used in Australia to label many rich and sweet dessert wines.

1 As of 1997 the use of French regional titles on Australian wines will become outlawed in accordance with Australia's new trade agreement with the E.E.C.. Hooray!

Food and wine

A STORM IN A WINE GLASS?

Some wine bibbers make a lot of huff and puff about this subject and I don't wish to detract from its importance to these individuals. Matching food and wine can in itself be a passion. However, to my mind the relevance of this subject is overstated. The reality is that if you start with a wine you like and you pair it with food of the same ilk, keeping in mind a few common sense rules, then it's pretty hard to be disappointed.

Naturally, if one is going to open a bottle of something very special, then it is well worth considering what food might best 'compliment' it. Ironically, any food, especially that served in a restaurant environment, will distract from the true nature of the wine, even when it compliments. If I have a very special wine to pull from my cellar, rather than pitting its subtleties against the amalgam of food, cigarette, perfume, after shave, etc aromas that fill a restaurant, I prefer to crack the bottle at home with a nice cheese plate or a delicately flavoured dish which will only serve as a backdrop to the wine.

Still I do find myself taking fine wines out to dinner and when I do, I will choose my food to compliment. There are certain flavour principles that dictate which food will compliment a wine and visa versa. However, there are really only two rules that need to be memorised:

RULE 1 : When matching food with wine think about weight of flavour ie: the richer the flavour of the dish, the richer the wine and vice versa. In the case of dessert style wines, sweetness may not be substituted for the use of 'richness' in the previous sentence. The reason for this is that a very sweet wine, when matched with an equally sweet dessert will be too cloying for most people's tastes. Many prefer to drink such wines with a strongly flavoured cheese (such as a blue-vein or a washed rind) or a fruit plate which has the acid to balance the wine's sweetness.

RULE 2 : Very spicy dishes, especially those containing chilli, will kill the flavour of most wines so there is no point going expensive. They can also make full bodied, tannic, reds taste bitter and hard. A full flavoured Riesling or Gewurztraminer, a chilled light-red, rose, or even a Sparkling Red can all work well. With ultra spicy/hot food it is difficult to find a better match than an ice cold beer, such as a Coopers Pale-Ale, although a fruity or semi-sweet white will often come close.

FOOD AND WINE MATCHINGS

(Please keep in mind that these are only suggestions. The opinions of so-called experts vary radically and the point is to experiment so that you can establish what suits your own tastes.)

WINE CODES:

Red 1 (Red Wines For Heroes pg 71)

Red 2 (Full Bodied Reds pg 79)

Red 3 (Elegant Reds pg 101)

Red 4 (Light reds & Rose pg 123)

White 1 (Full Flavoured Whites With Oak Influence pg 133)

White 2 (Crisp & Dry Whites pg 137)

White 3 (Perfumed & Dry - The Aromatics pg143)

Sweet 1 (Sweet & Sticky; The Dessert Wines pg 151)

Sweet 2 (Tokays & Muscats pg 159)

Sparkling (Sparkling Wines pg 179)

FOOD AND WINE MATCHINGS

Pasta	Bolognese and other meat based sauces.
Wine	Red 2
	Red 3
Pasta	Pesto, La Puttanesca, and other spicy sauces
Wine	Red 4
	White 2
	White 3 (Riesling)
Pasta	Carbonara and other cream based sauces
Wine	White 1
	White 2
Japanese	
Wine	White 2, 3
	Red 4
	Pork
Pork	
Wine	Red 3
	White 1, 3 (Riesling)
Vegetarian	Salads, asparagus, curries, steamed vegies
Wine	White 3
	Red 4
Soup	
Wine	Fino sherry (Consume) or
	Amontillado sherry (cream based soups),
	White 2
	White 3 (Riesling)

Red 1 (Red Wines For Heroes pg 71)

Red 2 (Full Bodied Reds pg 79)

Red 3 (Elegant Reds pg 101)

Red 4 (Light reds & Rose pg 123)

White 1 (Full Flavoured Whites With Oak Influence pg 133)

FOOD AND WINE MATCHINGS

Seafood	Full flavoured dishes such as Tuna, Mackerel, Atlantic Salmon, Ocean Trout, or any fish in a rich sauce
Wine	White 2 (Aged preferably) White 3 (Riesling) Red 3 (Pinot Noir)
Seafood	More subtle fish dishes, Oysters and other shellfish
Wine	White 2 White 3 (Riesling)
Seafood	Octopus, Marinara, Bouillabaisse
Wine	White 3 (Riesling)
Beef	Roast, BBQ, char-grilled, kebabs, casseroles, pies, sausages, Rissoles, etc
Wine	Red 1 Red 2
Lamb	"As above"
Wine	Red 1 Red 2 (especially Shiraz based) Red 3 (especially Shiraz based or a full flavoured Pinot Noir)
Chicken	
Wine	White 1 Red 3 (Pinot Noir)

White 2 (Crisp & Dry Whites pg 137)

White 3 (Perfumed & Dry - The Aromatics or The Aromatics: Full of Flavour, Yet Dry pg 143)

Sweet 1 (Sweet & Sticky; The Dessert Wines pg 151)

Sweet 2 (Tokays & Muscats pg 159)

Sparkling (Sparkling Wines pg 179)

FOOD AND WINE MATCHINGS

Chinese

Wine	White 3
	Red 4
	Red 3 (Pinot Noir)

Spicy Asian — Thai, Malaysian, Indian, Indonesian etc.

Wine	White 3
	White 2
	Red 4

Game Birds — Duck, Quail, Pheasant, Pigeon, etc.

Wine	Red 3 (especially Pinot Noir)
	White 1
	White 2 (Aged)

Game — Rabbit

	White 1
Wine	Red 3 (Pinot)

Game — Venison, Hare, etc.

Wine	Red 1
	Red 2
	Red 3 (a full flavoured Pinot Noir)

Veal

Wine	Red 3 (Pinot Noir)
	White 1

Pizza

Wine	Red 2
	White 1

Red 1 (Red Wines For Heroes pg 71)
Red 2 (Full Bodied Reds pg 79)
Red 3 (Elegant Reds pg 101)
Red 4 (Light reds & Rose pg 123)
White 1 (Full Flavoured Whites With Oak Influence pg 133)

FOOD AND WINE MATCHINGS

Desserts	Fruit cake, Chocolate based, etc	
	Sweet 2 (Especially Muscat)	
	Pudding, Creme Caramel,	
	Sweet 1	
	Sweet 2 (Especially Tokay)	
Desserts	Fresh fruits, Sorbet,	
Wine	Sweet 1	
	Sparkling or still Rose	
Desserts	Ice-cream	
Wine	Sweet 1	
	Sweet 2	
Cheeses	Cheddars and other hard cheeses	
Wine	Red 3	
	Red 2	
Cheeses	Soft ripened cheeses	
Wine	Red 3	
	Sweet 1	
Cheeses	Blue-vein and other stinky cheeses	
Wine	Sweet 1, 2	
Cheeses	Goats cheeses	
Wine	White 2	
	White 3 (Crisp Sauvignon Blanc)	
	Red 3	

White 2 (Crisp & Dry Whites pg 137)

White 3 (Perfumed & Dry - The Aromatics or The Aromatics: Full of Flavour, Yet Dry pg 143)

Sweet 1 (Sweet & Sticky; The Dessert Wines pg 151)

Sweet 2 (Tokays & Muscats pg 159)

Sparkling (Sparkling Wines pg 179)

Which wine?

A BUYING GUIDE UNDER STYLE HEADINGS

Due to style and quality variation, most wines that retail for less than ten dollars are not subject to classification in this listing. I have made some exceptions, yet generally speaking I have left it up to the reader to assess this cheaper price range for themselves either from newspaper reviews or from tastings. The accessible prices of these wines means that wine bibbers may experiment for themselves with a minimum of risk. Needless to say there are many bargains, as well as a few disappointments, to be found for an investment of less than ten dollars.

I have deliberately only included wines with which I am familiar and in which I have confidence in terms of their consistency of style and quality. I make no apologies for the absence of any wines, except to say that any future editions will be updated accordingly. As this listing of wines is based on my own personal experience, it should not, in any way, be taken as "gospel". Nor should it be surmised that a wine's absence from the pages of "Which Wine?" symbolises poor quality or that it is not worth buying.

Under "Which Wine", wines are grouped under their appropriate style headings and are given a review, which, in most cases, has involved a collaboration between myself and the wine-maker. This open affiliation between writer and producer is a unique concept, yet one that is not illogical. No wine writer can hope to have the same intimate knowledge of a wine as those who produce it. I have more or less acted as an editor inserting my own impressions where necessary and toning down any overuse of self praise. Where the wine makers have neglected to respond, I have included my own notes.

The wine style headings are descriptions of the wines at a young age. Naturally wines evolve with time and this is discussed, when appropriate, in the introductions to each style. For further insight into the phenomena of bottle development See page20.

HOW TO USE ' WHICH WINE?'

In this section of the guide, wines are reviewed under their appropriate wine style headings such as those listed below. This enables you to choose your wines not only in reference to quality, but also with regard to the food you will be eating, and, more importantly, what style of wine you are in the mood to drink. Simply select a style of wine from the list below and scan the following pages, titled on their fore-edge, for the appropriate section.

WINE CATEGORIES

- RED WINES FOR HEROES: (pg 71)

Rich and tannic wines for those after a powerful red.

- RICHLY FLAVOURED REDS, full bodied: (pg 79)

These wines are full flavoured with substantial weight of juicy fruit and firm tannins. They often exhibit substantial oak influence.

- RESTRAINED & ELEGANT REDS, full bodied: (pg 101)

Less overtly 'fruity' compared with the previous group, these wines also tend to show more delicate oak handling. They show immaculate balance of fruit, acid, and tannin in equilibrium, which makes them graceful drinking regardless of age.

- PINOT NOIR: (pg 123)

Soft and fleshy middleweight wines that at their best exhibit good intensity of flavour.

- LIGHT REDS AND ROSE: (pg 133)

Thirst quenching wines that typically show delicious berry characters and crisp acidity. Can be served chilled, although light reds can also be served at room temperature.

- CRISP & DRY WHITES: (pg 137)

These wines show an austerity of flavour in their youth, along with crisp acid and a streak of herbaceousness that makes them amongst the most refreshing of beverages. Predominantly unwooded Semillon.

- DRY RIESLINGS - A Class of Their Own: (pg 143)

Amongst our most delicious and interesting white wines. Full of citrus/floral zestiness in their youth, they will add toasty and intense lime flavours with time in the bottle. Riesling remains Australia's least expensive great wine.

WINE CATEGORIES

- PERFUMED & DRY - THE AROMATICS: (pg 151)

The Sauvignon Blanc and Classic Dry whites listed here have abundant fruit (gooseberry, tropical, grassy) aromas and flavours yet finish relatively dry, with zesty acidity.

- FULL FLAVOURED, DRY WHITES (pg 159)
WITH OAK INFLUENCE

Generally speaking, this category represents our most powerful and richly flavoured dry whites. These wines range from crisp, and restrained in flavour, to super rich, powerhouses of oak and viscous fruit.

- SWEET & STICKY, THE DESSERT WINES: (pg 179)

Rich and concentrated, sweet wines that show ripe apricot and spice aromas and flavours. Great with cheese and pate.

- TOKAYS AND MUSCATS: (pg 186)

Sweet, viscous dessert wines of the highest merit. The raisiny, chocolaty Muscats taste, literally, like liquid Christmas pudding and the more complex Tokays are blessed with the distinctive flavours of toffee and sweet, cold tea amongst other characteristics.

- SPARKLING WINES: (pg 189)

Not only for celebrating, all of the wines here make an ideal pre-dinner drink and some can work well with food.

See the beginning of each section (listed page numbers)

for complete descriptions.

For a complete index of the wine reviews in this section,

see pages 212-215.

RED WINES FOR HEROES

Rich and tannic red wines that in their youth will stand up to, and generally overpower, the richest foods. Enormous weight of viscous, mouth coating fruit can be expected here as can inky, astringent tannins that with time (around ten years) will begin to soften, and will be replaced with more complex, approachable flavours. In short, bottle age renders these wines more and more pleasant to drink. Some of the wines listed here will continue to improve in the bottle for 15 to 25 years, and some will live for many years more (see winemakers recommendations).

LEGEND OF SYMBOLS

"BM" - stands for bench-mark. Wines titles that are followed by this symbol are wines to measure others by.
"preBM" - indicates a wine that has shown itself capable of achieving a BM standard however the 'label' lacks either a long enough history of vintages or perhaps the consistency to be titled as such.
"V" - stands for Value. These wines represent very good examples of their region and/or wine style, and are relatively inexpensive (at least under $20).

*Baileys Shiraz (Formerly Classic Hermitage) (Glenrowan) V

An old favourite of many Australians and a flagship of Victoria's Nth East. This long lived wine typically shows rich, jammy fruit and inky, mouth drying tannins.

Aging potential: Needs at least five years to hit its straps and in good vintages can live up to twenty.
Greatest vintages still drinking well: '75, '79, '80, '85, '92, '93
Retail price: $14
Winemaker: Steve Goodwin

*Baileys 1920's Block Shiraz (Glenrowan) preBM

Typically a monster in terms of weight of fruit, alcohol and mouth gripping tannins. It has appeared more balanced in recent years, especially '93 which is the best young example of this wine that I have seen, exhibiting stewed plum and cherry fruits along with inky, tarry tannins.

Aging potential: Needs at least 10 years and in good vintages will live comfortably for 20 years and beyond.
Greatest vintages still drinking well: '75, '79, '80, '85, '92, '93
Retail price: $24
Winemaker: Steve Goodwin

*Bowen Estate Cabernet Sauvignon (Coonawarra) BM

A soft, fleshy wine that, despite the intense ripeness, and hence high alcohol content, shows no jamminess. Typically exhibits powerful cassis/plum like fruit and spicy, vanillin oak in support. One of Coonawarra's finest.

Aging potential: 8-12 years
Greatest vintages still drinking well: '84, '86, '87, '88, '90, '91, '92, '93, '94
Retail price: $19
Winemaker: Doug Bowen

Bridgewater Mill Millstone Shiraz (McLaren Vale/Clare) preBM

Ripe, jammy older style Australian Shiraz with great intensity of flavour (blackberry, ink\earth and some spice). Winemaker Brian Croser describes this wine as; "Simple impression of the best of Australian Shiraz and sunshine unmarred by [the] vanilla [flavour of] American oak."

Aging potential: 10 - 20 years
Greatest vintages still drinking well: '92, '93
Winemaker's food match: Steak, beef dishes.
Retail price: $18
Winemaker: Brian Croser

Chateau Tahbilk Old Vines (Goulburn Valley) BM

Traditionally exhibits pepper, earth and spice aromas with concentrated flavours of aniseed, earth and plum confined within a huge tannic structure. The finish is long and flavoursome and the wine is noted for its overall balance (that is, all components are equally massive!). This wine throws a heavy crust and is therefore in need of decanting prior to serving.

Aging potential: Average to good vintages 10-15 years. Good vintages 15-20 years. Great vintages 20 years+.
Greatest vintages still drinking well: '81, '84, '86, '91
Winemaker's food match: White and red meats, cheese and pasta.
Retail price: $60
Winemaker: Alister Purbrick

Technical data: Produced from Pre-Phylloxera, ungrafted vines planted on the estate in 1860. These grapes are destemmed before crushing; cooled to 10ºC and pumped into century-old, open oak fermenters where a cultured yeast addition takes place. The fermenting juice is pumped over skins once a day for 20 mins and drained off skins between 2 and 4 baume into large French oak barrels where fermentation is completed. Maturation takes place in oak for 18 months prior to bottling.

*Dalwhinnie Moonambel Cabernet (Pyrenees) BM

Typically exhibits a Bordeaux like aroma of Cassis and pencil shavings. The palate is substantial with cassis and plum like fruit, cedary oak and firm tannins. Regional mint character surfaces in some vintages. A powerful wine for the cellar.

Aging potential: 6 - 15 years depending on vintage. To be safe try a bottle between 6 and 8 years.
Greatest vintages still drinking well: '85, '86, '88, '88, '90, '91, '92, '94
Retail price: $28
Winemaker: Don Lewis

*Dalwhinnie Moonambel Shiraz (Pyrenees) BM

Another great Shiraz to dampen the spirits of our soul brothers in the Rhone. Typically exhibits intensely concentrated and complex Shiraz fruit with a streak of mint, firm tannins and great length.

Aging potential: 8-15 years
Greatest vintages still drinking well: '82, '86, '88, '90, '91, '92, '94
Retail price: $19
Winemaker: Don Lewis

*Jasper hills Emily's Paddock Shiraz-Cabernet Franc (Heathcote) BM

This winery only produces one style of red: powerful and long lived. Whilst these wines need at least ten years before their chewy tannins subside, their is plenty of red berry/ plum flavour and complexity to make them enjoyable in their youth.

Aging potential: 10 years +
Greatest vintages still drinking well: '85, '86, '88, '90, '91, '92, '93, '94
Retail price: $49
Winemaker: Ron Laughton

*Jasper hills Georgia's Paddock Shiraz (Heathcote) BM

Tends to show more overt vanillin characters and inky, earthy complexity than its more expensive brother. A complex and very classy wine.

Aging potential: 10 years +
Greatest vintages still drinking well: '85, '86, '88, '90, '91, '92, '93, '94
Retail price: $30
Winemaker: Ron Laughton

Jim Barry "The Armagh" Shiraz (Clare Valley) BM

This wine is generally "black" in colour with rich fruit aromas and inky tannins. In the mouth the wine is huge in every respect, with intense Shiraz (plums and spice) and vanillin oak flavours. Despite its weight, the wine is round and approachable in its youth with soft tannins and a lingering finish.

Aging potential: 10 years +
Greatest vintages still drinking well: '87, '89, '90, '92
Winemaker's food match: Red meat such as fillet or T-bone steak, all beef dishes.
Retail price: $75
Winemaker: Mark Barry.

Technical data: Sourced from a single vineyard from a unique clone of Shiraz vine that arrived in Australia in the 1960's. In the unirrigated vineyard the vines are left with 60 buds at pruning which gives 6 to 7 tonnes\hectare. The wine is fermented, slowly and comfortably, over a three week period then moved to new American oak barrels which are made in France (Mark Barry believes the French season the oak better) where it rests for around twelve months.

Penfolds Bin 707 Cabernet Sauvignon BM

(Predominantly Coonawarra & Barossa)
The Cabernet Sauvignon version of 'Grange', this wine is extremely rich and concentrated. Although 707s often shows plenty of the 'coconutty' sweetness of American oak in their youth, this settles down with time. Loads of ripe cassis and plum characters are typical as are firm grippy tannins.

Aging potential: generally needs 10 years to start hitting its straps but the better vintages will improve for many years more.
Greatest vintages still drinking well: '64, '76, '82, '83, '86, '87, '88, '90, '91, '93 (707 was not produced from the 1970 to 1975 vintages)
Winemaker's food match: Richly flavoured red meat dishes, soft cheeses, old cheddar.
Retail price: $60
Winemaker: John Duval

Technical data: Matured in new American hogsheads for around 18 months.

Penfolds Grange Hermitage (SA predominantly Barossa) BM

Massively concentrated and complex, Grange invariably needs 15 to 20 years to hit its peak. Don't get me wrong. you can drink Grange when it is relatively young, and many do when it is released at 5 years of age, but you had better be in the mood for "the mother of all wines". Needless to say, a mature Grange from a fine vintage is one of the great epicurean experiences.

Aging potential: Best drunk with at least 12 years of age and great years will live and improve well beyond 30.
Greatest vintages still drinking well: '53, '55, '62, '63, (some bottles may be passed their best) & '66, '71, '76, '78, '80, '81, '83, '86, '88, '90, '91.
Winemaker's food match: Richly flavoured red meat dishes.
Retail price: Around $140 on release (Although the '90 & '91 releases were sold by some retailers for over $300 a bottle).
Winemaker: John Duval

Technical data: Grange is a Shiraz yet in some vintages a small amount of Cabernet Sauvignon (up to 15%) may be used. The wine finishes its fermentation in new American oak hogsheads (300 litre) were it matures for a further 18 to 24 months.

Rosemount Balmoral Syrah [Shiraz] (McLaren Vale) BM

Formerly labelled "Show Reserve Syrah".
This wine's intense colour is matched by its powerful and complex aroma and flavour. The palate is typically richly flavoured (Plum, licorice, clove and cinnamon spice and a gamy edge of roasted meat) with a rounded mouthfeel, soft tannins, and a sweet complex finish that scents the breath for minutes afterwards. Oak character is evident yet it genuflects before the fruit.

Aging potential: Cellar for 5 years and drink over the following 15 years.
Greatest vintages still drinking well: '89, '90, '91, '92, '93
Winemaker's food match: Duck cooked in fruit and pepper sauce, smoked duck, game, red meats, or anything in a very rich sauce.
Retail price: $50
Winemaker: Philip Shaw

Technical data: 100% McLaren Vale Shiraz grown on light sandy soil overlying gravel clay. Aged for nearly two years in new American oak.

Wendouree Cabernet Sauvignon (Clare Valley) BM

Wendouree consistently produces reds of impenetrable colour, great depth of fruit concentration and a suppleness that belies the wine's power. This wine characteristically exhibits pristine Cabernet fruit flavours (blackcurrant) with some raspberry and subtle oak flavours of mint, vanilla and chocolate (becomes tobacco with bottle age). Fresh, lively acidity, firm tannins, and all components in harmony are the norm here as is a long, lingering finish.

Aging potential: 15-20 years
Greatest vintages still drinking well: '90, '91, '92, '94
Retail price: $30
Winemaker: Tony Brady

Technical data: The fruit is dry-grown (non irrigated) and hand picked, and the vines are hand pruned. The wine is basket pressed, open fermented with plunging, and matured in French oak hogsheads for 12 to 15 months.

Wendouree Pressings (Clare Valley) BM

A full bodied dry wine, dark in colour and rich in fruit flavours with very firm, fine, dusty tannins on the finish. Dark and brooding, it shows none of the porty characters often encountered in wines of this weight. A huge yet beautifully balanced wine that will live for many years.

Aging potential: With some breathing the wine can be enjoyed in its youth for its sheer power, or bottle aged to achieve softening. It will live and develop for a good 20 years.
Greatest vintages still drinking well: '75, '76, '77, '80, '85, '87, '88, '89
Winemaker's food match: Cheese, game, and red meats.
Retail price: The last vintage produced of this wonderful wine was 1989. Ironically, as many winemakers are making there wines softer and earlier drinking in style, Wendouree has found a growing demand for more weight and power in their reds. As a result, recent "pressings" have been blended back into their Cabernet releases. I include this note for those with wines in their cellar and in hopeful anticipation of future releases.
Winemaker: Tony Brady

Technical data: The early releases were made from blends of Cabernet Sauvignon, Shiraz, Malbec, and Mataro while later wines comprised of Cabernet Sauvignon\Mataro blends. In 1989 the Pressings were 100% Cabernet Sauvignon. The grapes that go into this wine come from very old, dry grown (unirrigated) vines that are very low bearing, giving small berries of grapes that have a great intensity of flavour, good levels of acid, low pH, and around 13% alcohol. The gentle action of the basket-press on the grapes makes the Pressings a rich and balanced wine. The wine is open fermented and plunged, to give good extraction, and spends around 12-15 months in a mixture of French and American oak hogsheads of which 20-25% are new each vintage.

Wendouree Shiraz (Clare Valley) BM

A full bodied wine that typically exhibits intense plum-like fruit and spice (pepper and cinnamon) flavours. The vintage variations are expressed from year to year as a deviation in the weight of the wine, and accordingly the intensity of colour and tannin. Firmer and more tannic wines are produced in dry years, and softer and rounder wines in the cooler years with good rainfall. The oak characters are typically in total harmony with the rest of the wine and are expressed in very subtle nuances of vanilla, coffee, tobacco and mint. A massively proportioned wine that, due to perfect balance, is supple and approachable in its youth.

Aging potential: 8-10 years
Greatest vintages still drinking well: The winery lists 1983 as the single greatest vintage for this wine. Well cellared bottles from 1970 onwards should still be drinking well.
Winemaker's food match: Cheeses, game and red meats.
Retail price: $26
Winemaker: Tony Brady

Technical data: The grapes that go into making this wine are grown on shallow red soils overlapping limestone. The vines are exposed to hot summers and drying winds that encourages early ripening grapes that retain high levels of natural acid. They are not irrigated but rely only on natural rainfall, hence variations in yearly rainfall contributes to vintage variation. The fruit is generally small berried with concentrated colour, flavour, acid and tannin. The wines are open-fermented with plunging and matured in oak (20% new).

Wendouree Shiraz Mataro (Clare Valley) BM

Although this wine is lighter in body, softer, and more forward drinking than the straight Shiraz from this producer, it is by no means a light wine. Rather, it is a richly flavoured, highly aromatic wine with great depth of plummy fruit and soft, chewy tannins.

Aging potential: 2-7 years (Will live much longer)
Greatest vintages still drinking well: Remarkably consistent. The winery lists 1992 as the single, post 1980, greatest vintage for this wine. Well cellared bottles from 1970 onwards should still be drinking well.
Winemaker's food match: Cheeses, game and red meats
Retail price: $20
Winemaker: Tony Brady

Technical data: The Shiraz\Mataro is sourced from a cooler position than the straight Shiraz, with deep alluvial soils giving later ripening wines of great flavour and softness. The Mataro grapes are sourced from bush vines planted in 1920 - the small canopies that result allow for the development of intense flavour, colour, and good tannins. The Mataro is used in the blend for its tannin content and the complexity it brings to this wine.

Wynns John Riddoch Cabernet Sauvignon (Coonawarra) BM

Unashamedly rich and tannic in all years this wine represents only the best of Wynns Cabernet Sauvignon from any given vintage. Typically exhibits the classic fruit characteristics of Coonawarra Cabernets (cassis & blackberry) along with inky tannins and plenty of sweet & soft vanillin oak complexity.

Aging potential: At its best with at least 10 years of age although the finest vintages will improve for at least two decades. If you are one of the few fortunate people to have some of the '82 in your cellar then try to avoid drinking this before 2000. It is one of the great Australian Cabernets.

Greatest vintages still drinking well: All vinatges so far produced represent excellent drinking and show no signs of tiring. The finest years are: '82, '86, '90, & '93

Winemaker's food match: When young this wine goes well with roasted or char-grilled red meats and soft cheeses. With age it is best complimented by 'saucy' red meat dishes, game, and mature cheeses.

Retail price: $70

Winemaker: Peter Douglas

Technical data: The majority of the fruit for this wine is sourced from very old vines grown on high limestone ridges. Vine vigour is low which accounts for the richness and intensity of the wine. Oak plays a significant role. The wine is matured in 100% new French oak for up to 26 months. No bottling is done if the wine is not going to achieve benchmark status.

Other Recommended Producers: Balgownie (Cabernet), Bullers, Campbells (Barkley Durif), Chambers, Morris, Taltarni ('Reserve' wines and back vintages of the Cabernet), amongst others.

RICHLY FLAVOURED REDS - *full bodied*

More "approachable" than the previous listing, these wines are full of flavour with good weight of fruit and firm tannins, yet these tannins are not so powerful as to mask the fruit. These wines will typically, though not always, exhibit substantial oak characters and they will benefit with age, complexity and elegance supplanting the exuberance of youth. Generally drinking at their best between five and ten years of age, although many will live and improve for considerably longer periods (see wine makers' recommendations).

LEGEND OF SYMBOLS

"BM" - stands for bench-mark. Wines titles that are followed by this symbol are wines to measure others by.

"preBM" - indicates a wine that has shown itself capable of achieving a BM standard however the 'label' lacks either a long enough history of vintages or perhaps the consistency to be titled as such.

"V" - stands for Value. These wines represent very good examples of their region and/or wine style, and are relatively inexpensive (at least under $20).

"*" - the author has compiled this wine description with little if any feed-back from the producer.

*Andrew Garret Shiraz (Multi regional blend SA) V

The last few vintages of this wine have represented tremendous value for money. Spicy berry and chocolate characteristics are typical as are firm tannins on the finish.

Aging potential: Should peak between 5 and 10 years
Greatest vintages still drinking well: '90, '91, '92, '93, '94
Retail price: $13
Winemaker: Phil Rescke

*Bowen Estate Shiraz (Coonawarra) BM

Few producers can make such a balanced, supple wine with grapes of this ripeness. This ultra ripe Shiraz is typically oozing with rich, earthy Shiraz characters, firm tannins, and a fair whack of oak all perfectly integrated. A robust yet classy wine that will improve with age.

Aging potential: Generally best between 5 and 10 years of age although can live longer.
Greatest vintages still drinking well: '87, '90, '92, '93, '94
Retail price: $18
Winemaker: Doug Bowen

*Brokenwood Graveyard Vineyard Shiraz (Lower Hunter Valley) BM

One of the finest reds of the Hunter, this wine typically exhibits ripe, plummy fruit and a hint of earth along with some subtle vanillin oak characters. A concentrated red wine of the highest order.

Aging potential: Drinks well when young however shows its best from around 8 years onwards.
Greatest vintages still drinking well: '83, '86, '88, '89, '91, '93, '94
Winemaker's food match: Red meat dishes especially lamb and game.
Retail price: $40
Winemaker: Iain Riggs

Cape Mentelle Cabernet Sauvignon (Margaret River) BM

A rich intense dry red that typically exhibits great concentration of flavour and length of palate. Blackberry fruit characters are emphasised, well integrated toasty, vanillin oak, and a long, chalky finish.

Aging potential: 10 years+
Greatest vintages still drinking well: '78, '81, '82, '83, '86, '88, '90, '91, '92, '93
Winemaker's food match: Aged beef and aged cheeses.
Retail price: $40
Winemaker: David Hohnen & John Durham

Cape Mentelle Shiraz (Margaret River) BM

A concentrated dry red usually showing plum, spice and pepper characters and firm chewy tannins. In some years a distinct aniseed character is evident.

Aging potential: 10 years +
Greatest vintages still drinking well: '83, '86, '89, '90, '91, '92, '93
Winemaker's food match: Squab risotto
Retail price: $18
Winemaker: David Hohnen & John Durham

Technical data: A partial whole berry fermentation with maturation in large oak casks allows fruit characters to dominate.

Cape Mentelle Zinfandel (Margaret River) BM

Cape Mentelle's "Zin" is a robust, zesty dry red with distinctive spicy, berry characters. High alcohol (typically 14%) gives the impression of sweetness in the middle palate but the finish is dry. Could be likened to a riper style of Shiraz.

Aging potential: 10 years +
Greatest vintages still drinking well: '81, '83, '84, '88, '90, '91, '93
Winemaker's food match: Lamb Korma and other spicy meat dishes.
Retail price: $18
Winemaker: David Hohnen and John Durham

*Chapel Hill Cabernet Sauvignon (McLaren Vale/Coonawarra) preBM

This wine typically exhibits a rich and smooth mouthfeel with the flavours of red berries and chocolate as well as some spicy/toasty oak. It is a powerful wine that will benefit from cellaring yet the wine's opulence tempts early drinking.

Aging potential: 5 years+
Greatest vintages still drinking well: '89, '90, '91, '92, '93, '94
Retail price: $20
Winemaker: Pam Dunsford

*Chapel Hill Shiraz (McLaren Vale) preBM

A richly flavoured soft and spicy Shiraz that typically exhibits plum like flavours and aromas along with a trace of the earth and chocolate characters for which this region's reds are famous.

Aging potential: 8 - 12 years
Greatest vintages still drinking well: '90, '91, '93, '94
Retail price: $16
Winemaker: Pam Dunsford

*Charles Melton "Nine Popes" (Barossa Valley) BM

"Nine Popes" typically exhibits raspberry/plum fruit characters, a touch of gaminess, dusty tannins, and warm, sweet alcohol. The '94 vintage shows more overt oak that lends the wine charred, vanillin nuances. Wonderful, complex drinking.

Aging potential: 5-10 years
Greatest vintages still drinking well: '90, '91, '92, '93, '94
Retail price: $19
Winemaker: Charles Melton

RICHLY FLAVOURED REDS - full bodied

Chateau Tahbilk Cabernet Sauvignon (Goulburn Valley) V

The wine traditionally exhibits great depth of complex fruit flavours (Cassis, tobacco, spice, with underlying mint and anise) matched by firm tannins and acid. It is a wine of the old school that is built to last. Would have previously been listed under the "Red Wines for Heroes" section but recent releases have been more approachable in their youth.

Aging potential: 10- 20 years depending on vintage.
Greatest vintages still drinking well: '64,'65,'66,'67,'68,'71,'76 - '79,'81,'86,'91
Winemaker's food match: white and red meats, pasta and cheese.
Retail price: $13
Winemaker: Alister Purbrick

Technical data: 90% Cabernet Sauvignon, 10% Cabernet Franc. Vines are an average age of 40 years. The wine is made in a traditional method. See Chateau Tahbilk Shiraz for more details.

Chateau Tahbilk Shiraz (Goulburn Valley) V

Typically shows a distinctive mixture of mint and anise fruit characters combined with pepper and spice overtones, substantial tannins and a lengthy, flavoursome finish. Would have previously been listed under the "Red Wines for Heroes" section but recent releases have been more approachable in their youth.

Aging potential: 10 to 20 years+ depending on vintage
Greatest vintages still drinking well: '71, '76, '77, '78, '79, '81, '86, '91
Winemaker's food match: white and red meats, pasta, and cheese.
Retail price: $13
Winemaker: Alister Purbrick

Technical data: The Shiraz grapes used to make this wine come from 40 year old vines (on average). Grapes are destemmed prior to crushing; immediately cooled to 10degrees and pumped into century old open oak fermenters where an addition of cultured yeast begins fermentation. The fermenting juice is pumped over skins once a day for twenty minutes and drained off skins between 2 and 4 baume to large French oak barrels where fermentation, both primary and Malo-lactic, is completed. Total time on skins is approximately 6-9 days. Maturation takes place in oak for 18 months prior to bottling. The wines are not fined and receive a pre bottling sterile filtration only).p

Elderton "Command" Shiraz (Barossa Valley) preBM

A richly flavoured, soft wine showing ripe Shiraz (plum, leather, earth) characteristics along with well integrated oak (vanillin, tobacco, spice). Reflective of James Irvine's immense talent as a winemaker.

Aging potential: The wine is released as a fully mature wine. Command Shiraz should live around 15 years.
Greatest vintages still drinking well: '88, '90, '92,
Winemaker's food match: Fully matured cheddar, stilton, etc. Game and beef dishes.
Retail price: $30
Winemaker: James Irvine

Technical data: The vineyard from which the grapes are sourced is part river alluvial and part red earth over limestone. The vines are fifty+ years of age and are late ripening. Each vintage the best barrels of Elderton Shiraz are reserved for further maturation and inclusion in the "Command" blend. The additional time in barrel concentrates the fruit flavours while adding complexity to the wine. The wine is matured in a mixture of 3\4 American oak (vanilla, tobacco) and (1/4) French, high toasted oak (spiciness).

*Hanging Rock Heathcote Shiraz (Bendigo) preBM

A rich, smooth red that has quickly established itself as a benchmark. Typically packed with plum and cassis flavours and a hint of earth. Highly recommended.

Aging potential: 4-8 years
Greatest vintages still drinking well: '90, '91, '92
Retail price: $35
Winemaker: John Ellis

*Hardys Eileen Hardy Shiraz BM

[Sometimes Cabernet] (Predominantly McLaren Vale and Padthaway)
The best red made by Hardys in any given year. The fruit can be sourced from a number of regions so style may vary, yet it is typically a solid wine with ripe fruit (plum and chocolate if Shiraz), vanillin oak (that needs a few years to fully integrate) and well integrated tannins. With time will typically develop into a wine of elegance and class.

Aging potential: Needs 5 years and will peak between 5 and 15.
Greatest vintages still drinking well: '82, '87, '88, '90, '91, '92, '93
Retail price: $26
Winemaker: Stephen Pannell

RICHLY FLAVOURED REDS - full bodied

Henschke "Cyril Henschke" Cabernet Sauvignon (Adelaide Hills) BM

Consistently outstanding in quality, this wine typically exhibits the characteristics of cassis and black-berry along with spicy/cedary oak and a hint of violets in certain years. A brilliant balancing act of power and elegance with ripe fruit flavours caged into a smooth and refined mouthfeel.

Aging potential: Lovely drinking when young (around 5 years) this wine will continue to improve for 8 to 10 years and will hold for several years afterwards.
Greatest vintages still drinking well: '83, '84, '85, '86, '88, '90, '91, '92, '93
Winemaker's food match: Lamb, veal and matured cheeses.
Retail price: $40
Winemaker: Stephen Henschke

Henschke Hill of Grace (Eden Valley) BM

Henschke is one of Australia's best known small producers and little wonder. For both consistency and sheer quality, the red wines of Henschke, challenge those of the venerable Penfolds stable. Ripe plum and spice Shiraz fruit flavours combine with the roundness and depth that can only come from very old, low yielding, vines (100 years plus in fact) and some sweet vanillin oak in support.

Aging potential: Needs 10 years and can comfortably live to twenty and beyond.
Greatest vintages still drinking well: '62, '80, '82, '84, '86, '88, '90
Winemaker's food match: Steak and kidney pie, red meats in a sauce, casseroles, game.
Retail price: $60
Winemaker: Stephen Henschke

Henschke Mount Edelstone (Eden Valley) BM

Most makers would be rapturous to have a Shiraz of this quality as their benchmark let alone their second in command. Whilst it may not have quite the depth and roundness of the 'Hill' it makes up for this with a vibrant intensity and an added pepper\spiciness to go with the ripe-plum like Shiraz and firm tannin/vanillin oak finish.

Aging potential: Drinks well from around five years and often peaks around ten.
Greatest vintages still drinking well: '62, '80, '84, '86, '88, '90, '91, '92, '93
Winemaker's food match: Charr-grilled or roasted red meats or game, soft cheeses
Retail price: $37
Winemaker: Stephen Henschke

*Hollick Coonawarra (Coonawarra) preBM

[Previously labelled Cabernet Merlot]
A supple, richly flavoured wine that typically exhibits the fruit characteristics of mulberry and redcurrants with vanillin oak and soft tannins.

Aging potential: In its youth, this wine represents soft, generous drinking yet it will benefit from around 5 years in the cellar.
Greatest vintages still drinking well: '89, '90, '91, '92, '93, '94
Retail price: $19
Winemaker: Pat Tocaciu

Howard Park Cabernet Sauvignon (Lower Great Southern) BM

Full flavoured, powerful, yet refined wine, with rich blackcurrant (cassis) flavours well married with new oak. A wonderfully intense yet balanced wine, made to cellar.

Aging potential: 15 - 25 years
Greatest vintages still drinking well: '86, '90, '91, '92
Winemaker's food match: cheese
Retail price: $45
Winemaker: John Wade

Technical data: 100% new oak enhances the wine. Skin maceration for 20 - 28 days promotes excellent colour and structure. In 1993, a small portion of the blend was sourced from the Margaret River.

Hugo Cabernet Sauvignon (McLaren Flat) V

Characteristically exhibits a bouquet of ripe berry fruits over rich supporting oak. The palate displays full, ripe mulberry fruit flavour with fine tannins, balanced with subtle French oak and a firm finish. Wonderful value.

Aging potential: 8-10 years
Greatest vintages still drinking well: '88, '90, '92, '93
Winemaker's food match: Red meats- beef dishes and most styles of cheese.
Retail price: $14
Winemaker: John Hugo

Technical data: Aged in French oak hogsheads (300lt) for a minimum of twelve months.

RICHLY FLAVOURED REDS - full bodied

Hugo Shiraz (McLaren Flat) V

Characteristically exhibits rich spicy Shiraz fruit characters with rich vanillin American oak. A wine with fleshy (mid-palate) fruit and fine soft tannins. Wonderful value.

Aging potential: 8-10 years
Greatest vintages still drinking well: 79, 86, 87, 90, 92, '93
Winemaker's food match: Red meat dishes such as Lamb and Kangaroo. Most cheeses.
Retail price: $ 15
Winemaker: John Hugo

Technical data: The Shiraz is aged for eighteen months in American Oak hogsheads (300 litres).

Ingoldby Cabernet Sauvignon (McLaren Vale) preBM

Ingoldby produces some of the finest reds in McLaren Vale. This wine typically exhibits berry fruits on the nose with a hint of mint leading on to a palate that is richly flavoured again with intense cherry/berry flavours and stylish, vanillin/ smoky oak. A full bodied wine of bountiful flavour and finesse.

Aging Potential: 10 years
Greatest vintages still drinking well: '80, '84, '86, '90, '85, '91, '87, '88, '89, '92, '93, '94
Winemaker's food match: Rare beef, meat dishes
Retail price: $17
Winemaker: Walter William Wilfred Clappis

Leo Buring DR 505 Cabernet Sauvignon (Coonawarra\Barossa SA) V

A richly flavoured Cabernet showing cassis and berry fruit flavours and aromas complexed by chocolate-like, vanillin oak characteristics and finishing with medium\firm astringency. Always outstanding value.

Aging potential: 6-10 years
Greatest vintages still drinking well: '88, '90, '91
Winemaker's food match: Red meat and matured cheeses.
Retail price: $15
Winemaker: Geoff Henriks

Technical data: The wine undergoes maturation for 15months in new and one year old American and French oak hogsheads.

McWilliams Barwang Cabernet Sauvignon (Young) preBM

This wine has typically exhibited blackcurrant/berry fruit, with traces of mint and cedary, well integrated oak. Winemaker Jim Brayne claims that there is a hint of leafy character to the wine that adds to its complexity. It is a big, intense wine but still elegant in structure and the palate is long with fine tannins on the finish.

Aging potential: 6-12 years
Greatest vintages: '91, '92, '93, '94
Winemaker's food match: Red meats
Retail price: $15
Winemaker: Jim Brayne

McWilliams Barwang Shiraz (Young) preBM

Typically shows the cherry/berry fruit character typical of a cool climate Shiraz supported by high quality integrated oak. The flavour in the mouth is rich and full yet the wine retains a fair degree of elegance. The last couple of vintages have pushed BM status. Remarkable value.

Aging potential: 10 years
Greatest vintages still drinking well: '89, '92, '93, '94
Winemaker's food match: Lamb, Cheese, Pasta
Retail price: $15
Winemaker: Jim Brayne

Mountadam Cabernet Sauvignon (Eden Valley) preBM

This winery is noted for producing refined wines with distinctive characteristics. The Cabernet is no exception, typically exhibiting a complex blend of blackcurrant, cedar and tobacco aromas on the nose followed by a palate that is rich and well rounded without any excessive oak sweetness.

Aging potential: 6-10 years
Greatest vintages still drinking well: '79, '84, '86, '87
Winemaker's food match: Venison, Beef dishes and cheese
Retail price: $25
Winemaker: Adam Wynn

RICHLY FLAVOURED REDS - full bodied

Mountadam "The Red" (Eden Valley) preBM

Typically a wine of great complexity and depth of flavour with the aromas and flavours of ripe plums and blackcurrant intertwined with gentle, high class oak. The high percentage of Merlot in the blend gives the wine a smoothness and great concentration in the middle palate. The wines produced under this label have thus far been of BM quality. With a few more vintages it seems certain to achieve this rating.

Aging potential: 6-10 years
Greatest vintages still drinking well: '91, '93
Winemaker's food match: Red meat dishes, cheddar cheese
Retail price: $30
Winemaker: Adam Wynn

Technical data: Made from 50% Cabernet Sauvignon & 50% Merlot, this wine is sourced from Mountadam's own low yielding vineyards. Matured in Troncais oak barrels.

Mount Avoca Cabernet Sauvignon (Pyrenees) preBM

In a region noted for red wines of power rather than elegance, Mount Avoca produces wines of considerable style and refinement. This wine typically exhibits good depth of fruit with sweet berry flavours that vary from vintage to vintage but are always present in different forms ie: strawberry, blackcurrant, raspberry. A slight trace of mintiness, a regional characteristic, is sometimes also perceived. Time in new French oak adds chocolate richness, spice, and soft tannins on the finish.

Aging potential: 4 - 10 years
Greatest vintages still drinking well: '88, '90, '92, '93
Winemaker's food match: Red meat, game dishes, and (according to Mathew Barry) Chocolate mousse.
Retail price: $18
Winemaker: Rodney Morrish

Technical data: The wine is a blend of Cabernet Sauvignon (sweet berry flavours), Merlot (soft finish, smooth and full mid palate), and Cabernet Franc (slightly spicy\game like characters). The wine spends nearly two years in new French oak prior to bottling.

RICHLY FLAVOURED REDS - *full bodied*

Mount Langi Ghiran Cabernet Sauvignon/Merlot (Grampians) BM

A rich, yet well balanced wine that traditionally shows soft fruit traits (berry, plums) a hint of stalky, herbaceousness and vanillin oak (always subtle and well integrated). Firm tannins and concentrated fruit flavours means that the wine needs time to show its best.

Aging potential: 10-15 years
Greatest vintages still drinking well: '86, '90, '91, '92
Winemaker's food match: Beef and other red meats.
Retail price: $19
Winemaker: Trevor Mast

Technical data: A blend of Cabernet Sauvignon, Merlot(25%), and Cabernet Franc(10%) which lends the wine a herbaceous character. Matured for 18months-2years in new French oak Barriques.

Mount Langi Ghiran Shiraz (Grampians) BM

A powerful, yet supple wine that typically exhibits spicy fruit characteristics and a deep crimson colour. A rich, mouth filling texture is to be expected along with well balanced acid, fine grained, soft tannins and a lingering finish. A brilliant example of a "black pepper", cool climate Shiraz.

Aging potential: Enjoy over the next few years if you prefer fresh fruit driven flavours, or cellar for the next 10-15 years to experience its potential.
Greatest vintages still drinking well: '86, '90, '91, '92, '94
Winemaker's food match: Beef
Retail price: $19
Winemaker: Trevor Mast

Technical data: Two years in New French Oak Barrels have softened the grape tannins and balanced the wine.

Orlando "Jacaranda Ridge" (Coonawarra) Cabernet Sauvignon BM

An excellent example of a rich, soft Coonawarra that typically exhibits cassis and ripe plum fruit, and in some vintages, such as '89, a herbaceous character. Extended maturation in new oak gives the wine nutty/chocolate oak flavours and aromas, chewy tannins on the finish, as well as granting the wine added complexity and softness.

Aging potential: 5 - 15 years.
Greatest vintages still drinking well: '82, '86, '88, '91
Winemaker's food match: Rich game or beef dishes.
Retail price: $35
Winemaker: Philip Laffer

Orlando "St Hugo" (Coonawarra) Cabernet Sauvignon BM

This wine continues to get better and better (Orlando claim the '90 is their best to date). Typically exhibits good depth of rich, dark berry characters integrated with cedary, smoky oak and firm chewy tannins on the finish.

Aging potential: 6-15 years.
Greatest vintages still drinking well: '85, '86, '88, '90, '93
Suggested food matching: Rich, full flavoured beef or game, roasts and stews.
Retail price: $18
Winemaker: Philip Laffer

Technical data: Matured in new French and American hogsheads for 20 months.

Parker Coonawarra Estate "Terra Rossa First Growth" (Coonawarra) BM

One of Coonawarra's most recent 'super premiums' this wine has entrenched itself among the elite of Australian Cabernets since its remarkable debut vintage of 1988. Typically a very concentrated wine with intense blackcurrant fruit and charry/ chocolate-like oak characters. It has substantial, yet fine, tannins, huge weight of fruit, and the overall balance for the long haul in the cellar.

Aging potential: 10 -20 years.
Greatest vintages still drinking well: '88, '90, '91, '93, '94
Retail price: $40
Winemaker: Ralph Fowler

Penfolds Bin 28 "Kalimna" preBM
(Barossa Valley, Clare Valley, McLaren Vale, & Langhorne Creek)

Another concentrated Shiraz from the Penfolds stable that typically exhibits plum and cherry fruit flavours encased in inky tannins. Perfectly ripened fruit is a key factor in this robust and unashamedly traditionally styled red.

Aging potential: Usually peaks around eight to ten years but great vintages can improve for fifteen to twenty years.
Greatest vintages still drinking well: '71, '77, '80, '83, '86, '90, '91, '92, '93
Winemaker's food match: Red meat dishes, casseroles, and richly flavoured, tomato based pastas.
Retail price: $16
Winemaker: John Duval

Penfolds Bin 389 Cabernet-Shiraz (SA muliti regional blend) preBM

Typically a fleshy wine exhibiting ripe varietal flavours of cassis, blackberries and red currants with the trademark inky tannins and charry oak handling.

Aging potential: 8-12 years. Great vintages will improve for decades longer.
Greatest vintages still drinking well: '66, '71, '78, '82, '86, '90, '91, '92, '93
Retail price: $17
Winemaker: John Duval

Penfolds Magill Estate Shiraz (Adelaide Metropolitan) BM

This is Penfold's alter Grange. Although a more refined and elegant style of Shiraz, in good years, this wine can match Grange for quality. The last few vintages have exhibited more concentration and power, and have typically shown supple, plum like characters with a hint of spice and vanillin oak beautifully married with the fruit. Needs cellaring.

Aging potential: Best drunk between 6 and 15 years.
Greatest vintages still drinking well: '83, '85, '86, '88, '89, '90, '91, '93
Winemaker's food match: Red meats, lamb casserole, soft cheeses and cheddar
Retail price: $40
Winemaker: John Bird

Technical data: A single vineyard wine made from Shiraz grown in Penfolds Magill vineyard near Adelaide. After partial barrel fermentation, the wine matures for 15 to 18 months in new American and French oak hogsheads.

*Penley Estate Coonawarra Cabernet Sauvignon (Coonawarra) preBM

Another recent addition to the brat-pack of Coonawarra 'super premiums'. Typically exhibits powerful Cabernet characters (blackberry/cassis) with top flight vanillin/spicy oak in support. Great depth of concentrated flavour packed into an elegant structure with dust fine tannins and a lingering finish. Seems certain to achieve BM rating with a few more vintages.

Aging potential: 7-15 years
Greatest vintages still drinking well: '90, '91, '93
Retail price: $35
Winemaker: Kym Tolley

RICHLY FLAVOURED REDS - full bodied

Petaluma Coonawarra (Coonawarra) BM

A pristine example of the best of Australian Cabernet with cassis, red currant fruit flavours, charred oak (spicy, vanillin) characters and soft tannic structure. Manages to balance depth of flavour with a restrained and elegant structure.

Aging potential: 8 - 20 years
Greatest vintages still drinking well: '79, '86, '88, '90, '91, '92, '93.
Retail price: $37
Winemaker: Brian Croser

Technical data: In the "Evans vineyard", mature Cabernet Sauvignon and Merlot vines are hand pruned. The wine is matured for two years in Nevers oak barriques and is bottled without filtration.

Peter Lehmann Shiraz (Barossa Valley) V

The winemaker's brief is to produce a Shiraz of full flavour (plum, chocolate, berry and occasionally mintiness) with rich oak flavours (vanilla\ coconut) and soft round tannins. It is accessible drinking when young yet it has the depth of flavour to ensure longevity.

Aging potential: 5-10yrs.
Greatest vintages still drinking well: '83, '88, '91, '92, '93, '94
Winemaker's food match: Red Meat, game and great cheese.
Retail price: $14
Winemaker: Peter Lehmann, Andrew Wigan, Peter Scholz and Leonie Lange.

Peter Lehmann "Stonewell" Shiraz (Barossa Valley) preBM

This is the flagship for Peter Lehmann Wines. Typically a wine of great depth and intensity of ripe, Shiraz characters, supported by generous, chocolaty oak. It is made to cellar for many years.

Aging potential: Released at 5 years of age and should live 20 plus years.
Greatest vintages still drinking well: All releases to date (Sept '96) have been of a very high standard.
Retail price: $40 (the '89 Stonewell Shiraz was released in Magnums for $100)
Winemaker's food match: Red meats, game and great cheese.
Winemaker: Peter Lehmann, Andrew Wigan, Peter Scholz and Leonie Lange.

Technical data: The grapes that are used to produce this wine come from low yielding, dry-grown, vineyards that are very old (some well over 100 years old). These vineyards are situated on the western slopes of the Barossa including such areas as Stonewell, Kalimna, Ebenezer, Moppa and Newkirch. The wine is fermented in new oak barrels and subsequently matured in these barrels for a further 2 - 2 1/2 years

RICHLY FLAVOURED REDS - full bodied

Pikes Cabernet Sauvignon (Clare Valley) preBM

A full flavoured yet soft wine that normally exhibits blackberry, black cherry and tobacco nuances with cedary oak in support. As with the Shiraz wines from this producer, there is often a delicious trace of mint in this wine.

Aging potential: 5-8 years
Greatest vintages still drinking well: '85, '86, '90, '91, '93
Winemaker's food match: Rich foods like beef, lamb, and game. Also good with cheese.
Retail price: $18
Winemaker: Neil Pike

Technical data: A small percentage of Cabernet Franc and Merlot is used to compliment the Cabernet Sauvignon component. The wine spends 18 months in French oak barriques.

Pikes Shiraz (Clare Valley) preBM

A full flavoured, soft Shiraz, very typical of the Clare, showing intense Shiraz fruit (blackberry\plum) and some sometimes spicy nuances. Pepper characters are only evident in cooler years. The oak is very much in the background yet adds complexity.

Aging potential: 5 - 8 years plus.
Greatest vintages still drinking well: '90, '91, '93.
Winemaker's food match: Most red meats and game. Also great with rich pasta dishes.
Retail price: $19
Winemaker: Neil Pike

Technical data: Pikes also release a "Reserve Shiraz", a rich spicy wine literally oozing with fruit and balanced wonderfully by a cage of inky tannins. If you are lucky to come across any, then it is well worth the extra $10 and would probably warrant a "BM" rating if it was reviewed.

*Riddoch Run Shiraz (Coonawarra) preBM

A delicious Coonawarra Shiraz that typically exhibits a soft and fleshy palate with plummy fruit and cinnamon like oak characters.

Aging potential: 4 - 6 years+
Greatest vintages still drinking well: '90, '91, '92, '93
Retail price: $17
Winemaker: John Innes

Rosemount "Diamond Label" Shiraz (McLaren Vale) V

A wine that typically shows the aromas of ripe Shiraz (berry\cherry, spice: cinnamon & clove, earth) and background oak that adds a smoky, toasty complexity. The palate is soft with plummy flavours and spicy oak. This wine typically shows a lovely balance and Philip Shaw's brilliant use of oak makes many other oak dominant Shiraz in this price range look clumsy. A pleasant "roast meat" character develops after 2 to 3 years. Terrific value.

Aging potential: Although ready to drink on release, Rosemount Shiraz achieves better balance with a few years bottle age and will hold for 5-8 years.
Greatest vintages still drinking well: '85, '90, '91,'92, '93, '94
Winemaker's food match: Thai beef salad, beef and pasta salad, roast pork loin.
Retail price: $14
Winemaker: Philip Shaw

Technical data: Fruit sourced from mature vines in McLaren Vale and small amounts from Mudgee (adds earthiness and complexity). American oak used.

Rosemount Show Reserve Cabernet Sauvignon (Coonawarra) BM

A richly flavoured yet balanced wine with cassis\berry fruit flavours, fine tannic grip, well integrated toasty oak characters and none of the stalkiness often attributed to this variety. Philip Shaw seems to be able to turn his brilliant winemaking abilities to the fruit of any region and come up with something special. This wine is no exception.

Aging potential: Hold for 3-5 years to allow the wine to reach maturity then drink over the next 10 years.
Greatest vintages still drinking well: '82, '86, '87, '90, '92, '93
Winemaker's food match: When young, these wines are best with rare or lightly cooked red meats especially steak and meat based soups. With age this wine suits more refined food such as Beef Wellington.
Retail price: $24
Winemaker: Philip Shaw

Technical data: The Kirri Billi vineyard in Coonawarra, where this wine is grown, is hand pruned and the grapes are hand harvested enabling more precise yield control, fruit selection and more even ripeness.

*Seaview Cabernet Sauvignon (McLaren Vale) V

This label nearly always represents outstanding value for money and the recent decision of Southcorp wines (Seaview's parent company) to increase the content of McLaren Vale grapes in the wine has meant even better quality. Typically soft and generous in flavour this is one of the few commercial reds that will benefit from bottle age.

Aging potential: 3-5 years
Greatest vintages still drinking well: '86, '88, '90, '91, '92, '93, '94
Retail price: $10
Winemaker: Mike Farmilo

Seppelt Dorrien Cabernet Sauvignon (Barossa Valley) BM

This wine has a characteristically complex, cedary bouquet with rich chocolate and blueberry like Cabernet fruit and charry, vanillin oak adding complexity and softness.

Aging potential: 10 years +
Greatest vintages still drinking well: '71 (Jimmy Watson winner), '86, '88, '89, '91
Winemaker's food match: Cheese, Kangaroo steak, an other red meat dishes.
Retail price: $28
Winemaker: Ian McKenzie

Technical data: The Dorrien vineyard's 7 hectares of vines are all Cabernet Sauvignon, some of them very old. There are a number of clones which may explain the wines complexity. The integration between fruit and oak flavours is partially due to 100% barrel fermentation and the wines age when released (usually 3 years). The wine spends 24 months aging in 100% new French oak prior to bottle aging.

*Sevenhill Shiraz (Clare Valley) V

Soft, flavoursome, unpretentious Shiraz that is quintessential Clare. That is, big in structure, yet supple.

Aging potential: 5-10 years
Greatest vintages still drinking well: '89, '91, '93
Winemaker's food match: cheese, roast lamb, other richly flavoured red meat dishes.
Retail price: $15
Winemaker: Brother John May

Taltarni Cabernet Sauvignon (Pyrenees) preBM

A strongly flavoured wine, full of inky tannins, dark fruit flavours, and chocolaty oak character in its youth. Not so long ago this wine would have necessarily been listed in the Red Wines for Heroes section of this listing, however, recent vintages have been more approachable when young. It is a wine noted for its longevity and better vintages will require many years in the bottle to show its best. Any 'Reserve' releases of this wine are well worth tracking down and are of "BM" quality.

Aging potential: 10-20 years
Greatest vintages still drinking well: '77, '78, '79, '82, '84, '85, '88, '90, '91, '94
Winemaker's food match: All roasted and barbequed meats, stronger cheeses.
Retail price: $19
Winemaker: Dominique Portet and Greg Gallagher

Technical data: Some Merlot and Cabernet Franc are used in the blend however it is predominantly Cabernet Sauvignon. Spends close to two years in oak (Nevers Barriques)

Taltarni "French Syrah" [Shiraz] (Pyrenees) preBM

A deeply flavoured wine with complexity derived from long maturation in oak. The ripe, soft fruit characters (berry, spice) are not however overwhelmed by oak flavours yet the powerful inky tannins may require several years of bottle maturation to allow the wine to truly express itself.

Aging potential: 10-20 years
Greatest vintages still drinking well: '78, '79, '81, '84, '85, '88, '90, '91, '92
Winemaker's food match: Roast Lamb and Beef, all barbequed meats, game dishes.
Retail price: $19
Winemaker: Dominique Portet and Greg Gallagher

Technical data: Often has a touch of Malbec in the blend, this wine spends close to 2 years in Nevers Oak Barriques prior to bottling.

Thistle Hill Cabernet Sauvignon (Mudgee) BM

This is typically a richly flavoured, fruit driven wine that in dry, warm years exhibits the characteristics of blackberry and chocolate while in wet, cool years, cassis and plum are most apparent. The wine exhibits the firm grape tannins and distinctive earthy nuances typical of the region

Aging potential: The wine is best drunk after 10 years when there is significant bottle age complexity to balance the rich, primary fruit flavours.
Greatest vintages still drinking well: '85, '86, '88, '90, '92, '93, '94
Winemaker's food match: Strongly flavoured dishes are essential to compliment this wine. Char grilled red meats with strong condiments and sauces are perfect with younger examples of this wine. Roast duck and most game dishes are great with aged examples.
Retail price: $20
Winemaker: David Robertson

Technical data: A single clone: SA125 is planted in the vineyard that produces flavours very true to the variety however regional characters and vineyard microclimate also play important roles. Approximately 40% of new oak is used each year. About 50% American and 50% French oak is used. Thistle Hill vineyard has a Grade A Organic Classification with the National Association of Sustainable Agriculture (NASAA)

*Tollana TR222 Cabernet Sauvignon (Eden Valley) preBM

Typically represents one of the better value cellaring styles on the market. Usually richly flavoured with soft and fleshy cassis/red berry fruit characteristics, spicy/vanillin oak and soft tannins on the finish.

Aging potential: 5-10 years.
Greatest vintages still drinking well: '86, '87, '88, '90, '91, '93, '94
Retail price: $17
Winemaker: Neville Falkenberg

*Wolf Blass "Classic Shiraz" Brown Label preBM (Premium SA regions)

Spicy, even peppery, red berry and plum Shiraz fruit flavours are typical along with good concentration of fruit to match the substantial, but not overpowering, spicy oak characters.

Aging potential: 6-10 years
Greatest vintages still drinking well: '83, '86, '87, '88, '90, '91, '92, '93, '94
Winemaker's food match: Red meat dishes, especially lamb.
Retail price: $19
Winemaker: John Glaetzer, Chris Hatcher

RICHLY FLAVOURED REDS - full bodied

Wynns Coonawarra Cabernet Sauvignon (Coonawarra) preBM

Typically exhibits rich cassis, blackberry and chocolate characters combined with charry/toasty oak. Chewy tannin structure and length of flavour are also the norm in better years.

Aging potential: All vintages will benefit from short term cellaring 3-5 years. Better vintages will improve for up to 15 years.
Greatest vintages still drinking well: '62, '70, '76, '80, '82, '86, '88, '90, '91, '93
Winemaker's food match: Red meats, hard and mature cheeses.
Retail price: $21
Winemaker: Peter Douglas

Yalumba Family Reserve Shiraz (Barossa Valley) V

Typically shows classic old-vine Barossa Shiraz characters of ripe plums with a sweetness coming from both the ripeness of the fruit and also the American oak used for maturation. Rich and velvety in structure with generous vanillin oak characters.

Aging potential: 8-10 years
Greatest vintages still drinking well: '88, '90, '92, '93
Winemaker's food match: Full flavoured foods, typically red meat dishes with rich sauces and matured cheeses.
Retail price: $12
Winemaker: Simon Adams

Technical data: Fully ripe Shiraz is sourced from dry-grown, low yielding (2 tonnes\acre) vineyards. These Shiraz vines are at least 60 years old. The wine is fermented at warm temperatures (partially in oak) and matured in American oak barrels.

*Yarra Yering Dry red No 1 (Yarra Valley) BM

Powerful, concentrated red that typically exhibits intense red currant and cassis fruit along with vanillin/cedar oak characteristics. Typically complex and very long in the mouth. One of Australia's finest wines.

Aging potential: 8-10 years
Greatest vintages still drinking well: '84, '85, '86, '88, '90, '94
Food match: Full flavoured foods, typically red meat dishes with rich sauces and matured cheeses.
Retail price: $40
Winemaker: Bailey Carrodus

Technical data: Predominantly Cabernet Sauvignon with some Merlot, Malbec, and Petit Verdot.

*Yarra Yering Dry Red No2 (Yarra Valley) BM

Typically an aromatic wine with a round, concentrated palate. Vibrant, plum like fruit is typical as are complex aromas and flavours that defy description. Nearly always represents wonderful drinking

Aging potential: 8-10 although good vintages should hold for several more years
Greatest vintages still drinking well: '83, '84, '85, '87, '88, '90, '94
Retail price: $40
Winemaker: Bailey Carrodus

Technical data: Predominantly Shiraz (at least 85%) with some Viognier.

*Zema Estate Cabernet Sauvignon (Coonawarra) preBM

The flavoursome and long lived wines of Zema Estate represent remarkable value. The Cabernet is typically bursting with essence like cassis and red berry fruits and toasty/chocolaty oak sweetness. The tannins are soft and the wine has a suppleness that defies its power.

Aging potential: 6-12 years
Greatest vintages still drinking well: '86, '88, '90, '91, '92, '93, '94
Retail price: $18
Winemaker: Matt Zema & Ken Ward

*Zema Estate Shiraz (Coonawarra) preBM

Typically a well balanced wine that exhibits good varietal characters of plum and spice with toasty oak in support and plenty of grip on the finish. Outstanding value for money.

Aging potential: 8-10 years
Greatest vintages still drinking well: '84, '86, '90, '91, '93 '94
Retail price: $18
Winemaker: Mat Zema and Ken Ward

RICHLY FLAVOURED REDS - full bodied

Other Recommended Producers: Chateau Xanadu, Clarendon Hills, Coriole, Grant Burge, Hollick Ravenswood, Irvine, Katnook Estate, Leconfield, Penwortham, Petersons, Pikes, Reynolds, Rymill, Saltram 'Mamre Brook' and 'No1', Turkey Flats, amongst others

RESTRAINED & ELEGANT REDS - *full bodied*

The Benchmark wines listed underneath show immaculate balance of fruit, acid, and tannin in equilibrium, which makes them graceful drinking throughout their lives. Such harmony tends to mask power and give the wine a delicacy, and sometimes an austerity of flavour, which often defies its chemical composition. These wines will often, though not always, have lower alcohol levels than the previous categories, but make no mistake, the benchmark wines listed here are not light reds, they simply show an extra refinement that makes them stand out from the crowd. They are generally at their peak between six and ten years (see winemakers recommendations) although some will live and develop for considerably longer periods.

In the case of the V wines below. The majority of these are in truth middleweights that are best drunk young whilst they are fresh and fruity.

LEGEND OF SYMBOLS

"BM" - stands for bench-mark. Wines titles that are followed by this symbol are wines to measure others by.

"**preBM**" - indicates a wine that has shown itself capable of achieving a BM standard however the 'label' lacks either a long enough history of vintages or perhaps the consistency to be titled as such.

"V" - stands for Value. These wines represent very good examples of their region and/or wine style, and are relatively inexpensive (at least under $20).

"*" - the author has compiled this wine description with little if any feed-back from the producer.

*Bannockburn Shiraz (Geelong) BM

A deliciously spicy Shiraz that seems to improve with every vintage. It typically shows a velvet-like mouth feel and a marked cinnamon spice character.

Aging potential: 5 - 10years
Greatest vintages still drinking well: '85, '86, '88, '91, '92, '94
Retail price: $19
Winemaker: Garry Farr

Bests Great Western Cabernet Sauvignon (Grampians) preBM

This great producer of Shiraz has shown itself to be equally deft with Cabernet Sauvignon. An elegant wine typically showing lingering flavours of "sweet" cassis and berry fruit along with cedary oak. Very close to BM status.

Aging potential: 10-12 years
Greatest vintages still drinking well: '88, '91, '92
Retail price: $18
Winemaker: Viv Thomson and Simon Clayfield

Bests Great Western Pinot Meunier (Grampians) preBM

This unique wine is produced solely from Pinot Meunier vines planted in the 1860's. The resultant wine is typically intensely flavoured with spicy, plummy fruit and an austerity in the mouth that belies its high alcohol and weight of fruit.

Aging potential: Drinks well young, the wine will continue developing for 15 years and in great vintages, live for up to 30 years.
Greatest vintages: '67, '69, '70, '75, '76,(well cellared bottles only) & '81, '88, '84, '92
Retail price: $20
Winemaker: E.V.Thompson & S.Clayfield

Technical data: The 'Concongella' vineyard's Pinot Meunier vines are considered to be amongst the oldest 'mother' vines in Australia. The wine undergoes a warm fermentation with the inclusion of some whole berries and stalks. Maturation is in old oak casks with a minimum of handling.

Bests Great Western Bin O Shiraz BM

[Previously labelled Hermitage] (Grampians)
A supple, rich and round Shiraz with generous berry flavours, soft tannins and well integrated quality oak. A complex, middleweight with just the right touch of vanillin oak and often a delicious trace of earthiness.

Aging potential: 8-20 years
Greatest vintages still drinking well: '77, '78, '80, '84, '85, '87, '88, '90, '91, '92
Retail price: $16
Winemaker: Simon Clayfield

Technical data: Exclusively produced from grapes grown on the Concongella vineyard. The wine spends two years in American oak puncheons prior to bottling.

Cape Clairault "Clairault" (Margaret River) preBM

Typically a soft, graceful wine with sweet fruit flavours (blackcurrant, spice, mulberry) and a hint of mint. The oak is well in balance as are the fine, dusty tannins. This richly flavoured yet elegant wine is quickly establishing itself as one of the finer reds in the Margaret River. The '91 is particularly stunning.

Aging potential: 10-15 years (although drinks well on release)
Greatest vintages still drinking well: '83 - '86, '88, '90 - '94
Winemaker's food match: In winter: Any rich meaty dishes. In Summer: Cheeses, rare steaks, fruit cakes.
Retail price: $22
Winemaker: Ian Lewis

Technical data: A blend of Cabernet Sauvignon, Merlot, and Cabernet Franc. 100% New French (Vosges) oak is used in the maturation of the wine and no pesticides are used in the vineyards.

Capel Vale Baudin (WA multi regional blend) preBM

This is a very difficult wine to categorise as the grape blend varies with each vintage. Typically however the palate is full flavoured and soft, with the fruit characteristic of plum and cherry, as well as exhibiting good integration of toasty, vanillin oak.

Aging potential: Can be enjoyed in its youth but will reward cellaring for 3-8 years.
Greatest vintages still drinking well: '85, '86, '87, '89
Winemaker's food match: Red meats, especially beef, and cheeses.
Retail price: $20
Winemaker: Rob Bowen

Technical data: Baudin is a blend of the finest parcels of red wine, made by Capel Vale in any given vintage. The '90 release for example was made up of 85% Merlot (Capel Stirling vineyard and Margaret River) and 15% Cabernet Sauvignon (Margaret River). Some years Shiraz and\or Cabernet Franc are included in the blend.

Capel Vale Shiraz (Capel/Mt Barker) V

A rounded, complex wine with blackberry fruit typically complimented by nuances of nutmeg and black pepper along with vanillin oak overtones.

Aging potential: 5-12 years
Greatest vintages still drinking well: '88, '91, '89, '92, '93
Winemaker's food match: Roast Lamb, Game
Retail price: $17
Winemaker: Rob Bowen

Cape Mentelle Cabernet Merlot 'Trinders V/yard' preBM (Margaret River)

A fully flavoured yet soft red with fine tannins, fresh berry and plum fruit flavours, and toasty\vanillin oak in support.

Aging potential: 3 to 8 years
Greatest vintages still drinking well: '92, '94
Winemaker's food match: Pasta and light red meat dishes.
Retail price: $17
Winemaker: David Hohnen & John Durham

Technical data: Vinified using traditional methods, including long maceration on skins and fourteen months maturation in Nevers oak Barriques, one third of which are new each vintage.

Cassegrain Chambourcin (Hastings Valley) V

A fully flavoured yet soft wine with a cleansing natural acidity on the finish. When young, the wine typically displays a plummy, spicy nose, often with a slightly herbaceous (green tomato) character. With bottle age the wine takes on a complex leathery character and more intense plummy characteristics, not unlike an aged Shiraz.

Aging potential: 3 - 10 years
Greatest vintages still drinking well: '86, '89, '93
Winemaker's food match: tomato based sauces, pasta dishes, pizzas, char grilled tuna or salmon.
Retail price: $16
Winemaker: John Cassegrain and Drew Noon

Technical data: 7 g/l of acidity, which is considered high for red wines, plays an integral part in this wine's structure and freshness. A portion of the wine goes through Carbonic Maceration which adds richness to the middle palate. Oak has played a minor role in the wines to date, however the winery is continuously experimenting and is slowly increasing the proportion of new oak treatment while carefully monitoring oak tannin extraction.

*Coldstream Hills 'Reserve' Cabernet Sauvignon (Yarra Valley) BM

A tremendous example of Yarra Valley Cabernet. Tightly structured in its youth it typically shows berry/cassis fruit characteristics, cedary oak and ultra fine tannins on the lingering finish.

Aging potential: Although delicious young, this wine needs at least 5-10 years to start showing its wares and can live considerably longer.
Greatest vintages still drinking well: '88, '90, '91, '92, '93, '94
Retail price: $35
Winemaker: James Halliday

*Craiglee Shiraz (Sunbury, Macedon) BM

This small winery is consistently producing some of Australia's finest cool climate Shiraz. Typically a rich and smooth wine with the classic aroma of freshly ground black pepper. Wonderful drinking.

Aging potential: Great vintages of this wine will live a long time, however it is my experience that they drink quite deliciously from around eight years onwards.
Greatest vintages still drinking well: '88, '90, '91, '93
Retail price: $24
Winemaker: Pat Carmody

Cullen Cabernet Merlot (Margaret River) BM

This wine has masses of fresh berry fruit flavours with a Bordeaux-like austerity in its youth as well as a cedar oak character. It is elegant yet full flavoured with a lingering finish that scents the breath for minutes after swallowing. Cullen also produce a 'Reserve' Cabernet Merlot which is nothing short of sublime.

Aging potential: 10-20 years
Greatest vintages still drinking well: '76 - '79, '82, '84, '85, '88, '90, '91, '92, '94
Winemaker's food match: red meats such as steak, cheese
Retail price: $25
Winemaker: Vanya Cullen

Technical data: A classic blend of Cabernet Sauvignon, merlot and Cabernet Franc.

*Delatite Devils River (Mansfield) preBM

A richly flavoured, fruit driven wine packed with cassis and plum fruits along with a minty streak, often described as eucalyptus or menthol, that is a trademark of Delatite's reds.

Aging potential: 10 - 20 years depending on vintage.
Greatest vintages still drinking well: '88, '89, '90, '91, '92, '94
Retail price: $18
Winemaker: Rosalind Ritchie

Evans & Tate Cabernet Sauvignon (Margaret River) preBM

This Margaret River Cabernet typically exhibits soft but full berry/spicy blackcurrant characters combined with gentle oak, fine-grained tannins and a lingering finish. A leafiness is apparent in some vintages. This elegant wine is sometimes richened by the addition of a small percentage of Merlot.

Aging potential: 7 years +
Greatest vintages still drinking well: '91, '93, '94
Winemaker's food match: To be enjoyed with full flavoured foods such as a blue-vein cheese or a fillet of Harvey beef.
Retail price: $22
Winemaker: Brian Fletcher

Evans and Tate Merlot (Margaret River) BM

Ripe plum, berry and tobacco characters typically combine with spicy oak and fine-grained tannins to create this supple and elegant wine. One of Australia's finest examples of Merlot.

Aging potential: 6-10 yrs
Greatest vintages still drinking well: '84, '90, '91, '92, '93, '94
Recommended food match: May be enjoyed with game dishes such as pheasant or water buffalo and is ideal with cheeses.
Retail price: $22
Winemaker: Brian Fletcher

Technical data: Produced from 100% Merlot, this wine is aged in new French oak barriques for 18 months. It is made very much in the Bordeaux mould, and following the practices of the Houses of Pomerol some 50% of the fruit undergoes prolonged skin contact to extract more of the flavour, colour and tannin from the skins.

Evans & Tate Shiraz [Previously labelled as Hermitage] (Margaret River) BM

A wine that traditionally exhibits rich fruit flavours (plums, spice, pepper), a smooth as velvet mouthfeel, and fine, dusty tannins. There are generous oak flavours yet these are in balance with the rest of the wine. Maturation in high quality French and American oak adds significantly to the wine's weight and complexity. A marvellous and underrated wine.

Aging potential: 5-8 years
Greatest vintages still drinking well: '90, '92, '93, '94
Winemaker's food match: Fillet of 'roo.
Retail price: $20
Winemaker: Brian Fletcher

Giaconda Cabernet Sauvignon\Merlot\Franc (Beechworth) BM

Typically exhibits the aromas of black fruits and cedary characters, this wine is extremely rich and voluptuous in the mouth, with fine elegant flavours. Very good length of flavour is the norm as are well integrated tannins.

Aging potential: This wine can be drunk when young but should improve for 5-10 years.
Greatest vintages still drinking well: '88, '90, '91, '92
Winemaker's food match: Traditional meat dishes & cheese.
Retail price: $26
Winemaker: Rick Kinzbrunner

Technical data: Cabernet Sauvignon 70% (gives structure power) Merlot 20% (gives fruit richness), Cabernet Franc 10% (gives finesse & aromatic character). The wine is aged for longer periods than most Cabernets spending 2.5 years in minimal new oak (10% or less). Traditional techniques used and the wine is bottled unfiltered.

*Goona Warra Cabernet Franc (Sunbury, Macedon) preBM

A delicious middleweight that typically exhibits spicy cherry\cassis characters and a lively acidity.

Aging potential: 2-6
Greatest vintages still drinking well: '91, '92, '93
Retail price: $18
Winemaker: John Barnier

*Goundrey Reserve Shiraz (Mount Barker) preBM

A wonderful wine that typically exhibits essence like fruit in the plum/cherry spectrum along with a streak of spice and that heady bouquet of violets, a regional characteristic of Mount Barker.

Aging potential: 3-6 years
Greatest vintages still drinking well: '91, '92, '93 '94
Retail price: $16
Winemaker: Brendan Smith

RESTRAINED & ELEGANT REDS - full bodied

Gramps Cabernet Merlot (SA multi regional blend) V

This wine has often been the star value red in Orlando's portfolio since its release in the mid eighties. It typically shows ripe dark berry and plum characteristics along with subtle vanillin oak (this subtlety being a rarity in inexpensive reds these days). It also has its fair share of complexity with earthy characters making it more interesting drinking than many other wines in this price range. Sadly, recent vintages have not quite been up to the quality of earlier releases.

Aging potential: 3-5 years
Greatest vintages still drinking well: '87, '88, '90
Winemaker's food match: Rich veal and Lamb dishes
Retail price: $13
Winemaker: Philip Laffer

Technical data: The fruit for this wine is sourced from Coonawarra, Southern Vales, Barossa Valley, Padthaway, and Langhorne Creek. The wine, a blend of Cabernet Sauvignon, Cabernet Franc, and Merlot, is matured in a mixture of American and French small oak casks.

Grosset Gaia (Clare Valley) BM

A delicious wine that is typically supple and perfectly balanced, with intense berry flavours, ultra fine tannins, and lingering flavour. Full flavoured yet refined, this wine is a tribute to the substantial winemaking skills of Jeffrey Grosset.

Aging potential: 8-15 years
Greatest vintages still drinking well: '90, '92, '93, '94
Winemaker's food match: Rich veal and Lamb dishes
Retail price: $25
Winemaker: Jeffrey Grosset

Technical data: Sourced mainly from Jeff's Gaia vineyards in the Clare Valley, at 570m. This wine spends 15 months in 100% French oak of which 40% is new.

Heggies Vineyard Cabernets (Eden Valley) preBM

The initial releases of this wine, '85-'90, were typically blends of Cabernet Sauvignon (60-70%) Cabernet Franc (10-15%) and Merlot (10-15%). These wines showed typical cool climate characters of tea leaf and cigar box when young and a fine acid backbone. In the mouth they were typically soft and fleshy yet restrained and in need of time to show their best. Future releases, '91 onwards, are more Merlot dominant and changes in the vineyard have seen, much riper fruit at harvest time. New releases, from '92 onwards, are substantially riper, fuller wines.

Aging potential: 4-6 years
Greatest vintages still drinking well: '88, '90
Recommended food match: When the wine is young, it goes well with Asian food, lighter red meat, and poultry dishes. When mature enjoy with matured cheeses.
Retail price: $18
Winemaker: Simon Adams

Technical data: All new vineyard plantings are close spaced, 1m x 1m. Barrel fermentation grants a richness to the wine and a balance of oak and fruit. Oak used: French Vosges.

*Hollick Ravenswood Cabernet Sauvignon (Coonawarra) BM

This wine is liquid Coonawarra refinement. This wine typically exhibits the fruit characters of cassis and red berries integrated brilliantly with smoky, spicy oak. It has the structure and weight to cellar over the long term yet also the balance that makes it delicious drinking on release.

Aging potential: Should peak around ten years of age.
Greatest vintages still drinking well: '88, '89, '90, '91, '92, '93
Retail price: $35
Winemaker: Pat Tocaciu

Huntington Estate Cabernet Merlot (Mudgee) V

A smooth reliable wine with good depth of cassis, plummy fruit and sweet vanillin oak. Lighter in body than the straight Cabernet and more forward drinking.

Aging potential: Should peak between 5- 8 years
Greatest vintages still drinking well: 84, 82, 86, 89,
Winemaker's food match: Any meat or poultry
Retail price: $15
Winemaker: Bob Roberts

Technical data: Merlot makes up 18-25% of the final blend.

Huntington Estate Cabernet Sauvignon (Mudgee) preBM

These wines are generally developed and complex in character with lifted aromas (red berries, earthy), full, rich flavours, (cassis, coffee, chocolate) plenty of chewy tannins and just the right touch of oak character. Can often outshine comparable wines at twice the price and at such times represents outstanding value.

Aging Potential: These wines are made to age around 10 years.
Greatest Vintages still drinking well: '79, '84, '86, '89, '90, '91
Winemaker's food match: Any meat or poultry
Retail price: $15
Winemaker: Bob Roberts

Technical data: Wine is 100% estate grown and 100% Cabernet Sauvignon and undergoes up to 2 years barrel aging.

Lake's Folly Cabernet Sauvignon (Lower Hunter) preBM

Typically an elegant, medium bodied wine which none the less contains the power to age well over many years. The palate characteristically exhibits sweet ripe berry fruits, soft tannins and subtle, spicy oak.

Aging Potential: 5-20 years. On average about 12 years.
Greatest Vintages: '69, '72, '78, '81, '87, '89, '91, '93, '94
Recommended food match: Winemaker Stephen Lake offers "no rules", simply saying that "enjoyment is the name of the game". When young, this wine will benefit from a decanting.
Retail price: $30
Winemakers: Stephen Lake

Technical data: Predominantly Cabernet Sauvignon with small proportions of Shiraz, Merlot and Petite Verdot (all estate grown). The fruit production (ie. tonnes per hectare) is kept low to maximise flavour, and the grapes are hand picked. The wine is open fermented and matures in French oak (Nevers & Troncais): 1/3rd new, 1/3rd one year old, and 1/3rd two year old.

Leeuwin Estate Cabernet Sauvignon (Margaret River) BM

I recently tasted every vintage from '89 onwards, including the '93 and '94 barrel sample, and I can confidently relay to readers that these are amongst the Margaret River's best Cabernets. They show great intensity and depth of flavour as well as a balance and complexity rarely seen in Australian reds. The palate is a model of refinement with ultra fine tannins and acid giving a structure and length of flavour hauntingly reminiscent of a top Bordeaux.

Aging potential: While the superb balance of these wines will ensure longevity it is my feeling. at this stage, that they will not greatly benefit from much more than 10 years in the bottle. Drinks well on release and ideally would be given 5-10 years in the cellar.
Greatest vintages still drinking well: '89, '90, '91, '92, (with '93 and '94 both promising a great deal in barrel)
Retail price: $24
Winemaker: Bob Cartwright

Lillydale Cabernet Merlot (Yarra Valley) V

A medium weight yet flavoursome wine which traditionally exhibits the aromas of plums, cassis and cherry. The palate is soft with fine tannins balanced by sweet, soft oak characteristics. In better years this wine can represent astounding value for money.

Aging potential: Drinks well on release, yet should peak between 4 and 8 years.
Greatest vintages still drinking well: '85, '86, '90, '91, '92, '94
Winemaker's food match: Goes well with Italian pasta and mild Sri Lankan Curries plus the usual steak and red meat dishes.
Retail price: $15
Winemaker: Jim Brayne.

Lindemans Hunter River Shiraz ["Burgundy"] (Lower Hunter Valley) V

A full flavoured, round and soft wine, that typically exhibits earthy Hunter flavours and aromas married well with the more common "plums and spice" Shiraz characters.

Aging potential: 10-20 years
Greatest vintages still drinking well: '59, '65, '80, '83, '87, '91
Winemaker's food match: Char-grilled red meats
Retail price: $19
Winemaker: Patrick Auld

Technical data: Matured in 2, 3, and 4 year old French (Allier & Vosges) and some American oak.

Lindemans Hunter River Steven Shiraz [Hermitage] (Lower Hunter) V

Full in flavour, with concentrated spicy and earthy flavours and aromas complexed by vanillin oak characters.

Aging potential: 10-12 years-in excellent vintages
Greatest vintages still drinking well: '79, '83, '87, '91
Winemaker's food match: Red meats
Retail price: $19
Winemaker: Patrick Auld

Technical data: The oak used for this wine is predominantly American with equal percentages of new, one, and two year old oak.

Lindemans Limestone Ridge Shiraz-Cabernet (Coonawarra) preBM

For mine, this is the best of the three premium Lindemans reds from Coonawarra. It is a fruit driven style that typically exhibits concentrated fruit flavours of plum and blackberry. It is soft and approachable in its youth but will benefit from medium term cellaring.

Aging potential: 6-10 years. Great vintages can improve over longer periods.
Greatest vintages still drinking well: '82, '86, '87, '88, '90, '93
Retail price: $30
Winemaker: Greg Clayfield

Main Ridge Cabernet Sauvignon (Mornington Peninsula) BM

Typically an elegant, fragrant, medium bodied wine. Soft, fine grained tannins and good acidity ensure longevity and with time a cigar box character typically develops to compliment the small berry fruit flavours and aromas (in the raspberry\blackcurrent spectrum). Oak completes the picture adding very subtle vanilla and coffee bean characteristics.

Aging potential: At least ten years although the wine drinks well when young.
Greatest vintages still drinking well: '80, '86, '90, '91 - '94
Winemaker's food match: Meat dishes, cheese.
Retail price: $22
Winemaker: Nat White

Technical data: Low yielding, non irrigated vineyard gives intensity and flavour at moderate ripeness (approx. 12.5% alcohol). Scott-Henry trellising is employed in the vineyard to give maximum ripeness. The wine undergoes a long maceration (24 days) and fermentation on skins in open vats. Malo-Lactic fermentation and maturation occurs in French oak barriques.

McAlister, The (Gippsland) BM

A finely structured, medium-bodied red whose balance and complexity make it superb with food. Elegant and refined are justifiable descriptions for The McAlister which typically exhibits berry flavours, earthy complexity and some fine tannin on the lingering finish. This wine ages particularly well.

Aging potential: Generally 6-10 years. In the great years; 15years.
Greatest vintages still drinking well: '84, '87, '88, '90, '91, '93, '94
Winemaker's food match: Compliments a wide variety of foods. In its youth- pasta, chicken, lamb, veal. When mature- roasts, game, pate.
Retail price: $27
Winemaker: Peter Edwards

Technical data: The McAlister vineyard is planted to the classic Bordeaux varieties of Merlot (30%) and Cabernet Sauvignon, Cabernet Franc, and Petit Verdot (70% combined). Winemaking is traditional, using naturally occurring yeasts, long cuvaison (fermentation with skins to extract colour and tannins), low sulphur, and oak maturation of up to 2 years in French (Nevers & Allier) oak barriques. The wines are egg-fined if necessary. They are not filtered. Great importance is placed on viticulture, the vines being subject to strict pruning and cluster thinning aimed at optimum fruit production.

Moorooduc Estate Cabernet Sauvignon (Mornington Peninsula) preBM

From 1990, with the help of maturing vines, the McIntyres have achieved more ripeness in their Cabernet and have also altered the winemaking practises to produce richer more complex wines. Whilst the emphasis remains on elegance, these later wines have excellent weight of flavour (blackcurrant, strawberry, spice), restrained oak characters, and soft yet persistent tannins. With wines of this quality so early in a vineyard's life, one cannot help but salivate at the thought of future treasures.

Aging potential: Will benefit from at least 3-8 years in the bottle and will live for at least ten years.
Greatest vintages still drinking well: '90, '91, '92, '93, '94
Winemaker's food match: Strongly flavoured meats such as beef, hare, and kangaroo.
Retail price: $23
Winemaker: Richard McIntyre

Technical data: Predominantly Cabernet Sauvignon with a small percentage of Merlot (10%) and Cabernet Franc (5%), all estate grown. In the vineyard, vertical shoot positioning and leaf plucking are practised to maximise fruit exposure. In the winery, the wine undergoes prolonged skin contact for an average of three and a half weeks. This practise contributes significantly to the wine's colour and weight. The wine spends two years in French Barriques with a proportion of new barrels each year and spends at least one year in bottle before being released.

*Moss Wood Cabernet Sauvignon (Margaret River) [Incl. Reserve] BM

One of Australia's greatest wines, typically restrained in style, its power is often masked by the wine's impeccable balance and soft mouthfeel. Packed with cassis and red berry fruit and smoky/spicy oak that is perfectly integrated, this wine can sometimes exhibit a subtle streak of mint or violets. In worthy vintages, Moss Wood release a tiny quantity of "Reserve" Cabernet Sauvignon. These wines have an extra dimension of power and fruit concentration as well as substantial, yet again well integrated, oak characters. One of my wine highlights of 1996 was drinking both the '83 and '91 vintages of the Reserve Cabernet. Both of these wines were nothing short of brilliant.

Aging potential: 10 - 20 years
Greatest vintages: '74, '75, '76, '79, '80, '83, '85, '87, '88, '91, '92, '94
Retail price: $30
Winemaker: Keith Mugford

Technical data: Predominantly Cabernet Sauvignon with a small percentage of merlot (10%) and Cabernet Franc (5%), all estate grown. In the vineyard, vertical shoot positioning and leaf plucking are practised to maximise fruit exposure. In the winery, the wine undergoes prolonged skin contact for an average of three and a half weeks. This practise contributes significantly to the wine's colour and weight. The wine spends two years in French Barriques with a proportion of new barrels each year and spends at least one year in bottle before being released.

*Mount Mary 'Quintet' Cabernets (Yarra Valley) BM

One of Australia's original 'cult' wines, this is a wine that well deserves its status. It is typically supple and juicy in its youth yet with an austerity and structure that can be discerningly like a fine Bordeaux. It is customarily a wine of complexity, exhibiting numerous fruit and oak characteristics. Of these, perhaps the most striking is the aroma of fresh violets that I have often found intertwined with the red berries/red currants and cedarwood of younger Mount Mary's. It is a wine of infinite refinement that strikes a perfect balance of all components ensuring the longevity for which is it noted.

Aging potential: In general this wine needs 8-10 years to truly blossom and will often live and develop for many years more.
Greatest vintages still drinking well: '78, '80, '82, '84, '86, '88, '90, '91, '92, '93
Retail price: $60
Winemaker: John Middleton

Oakridge "Reserve" Cabernet Sauvignon (Yarra Valley) BM

Although grown in a cooler climate this wine is full and rich and typically does not exhibit any green\herbaceous characters. It shows redberry\currant and blackberry fruit, a spiciness, and plenty of vanillin oak. It is produced only in the best vintages and is a wine that will repay cellaring. A stunning, concentrated example of Yarra Valley Cabernet.

Aging Potential: 12-15 years
Greatest Vintages still drinking well: '90, '91 (no 92, 93 made)
Retail price: $32
Winemaker: Michael Zitzlaff

Technical data: Mostly 100% Cabernet Sauvignon grown in the red soil of the Yarra, but some years such as 1991, 5% or 10% merlot or Cab Franc can be added. The wine spend almost two years in new French oak.

Penfolds Koonunga Hill Shiraz/Cabernet Sauvignon V

[Formerly Claret] (SA multi regional blend)
Probably the benchmark of wines around the $10 mark, this wine typically exhibits the complexity of flavour, balance and longevity that many other 'cheapies' lack. Blend and regions vary from year to year, yet despite this the wine has shown a remarkable consistency of style and quality. You can expect some degree of plum/berry fruit characteristics, a hint of spice and much more class than you would normally get in this price range.

Aging potential: 3-10 years
Greatest vintages still drinking well: '82, '86, '87, '90, '91, '92, '93, '94
Retail price: $10
Winemaker: John Duval

Plantagenet Cabernet Sauvignon (Mount Barker) preBM

Typically a rich and complex wine showing mulberry/blackberry fruit characters together with the cedar, mocha, chocolate characters of good French oak.

Aging potential: Although approachable when released, this wine benefits greatly from 6-10 years of bottle age and will live, in better vintages, for 20 years.
Greatest vintages still drinking well: '76, '77, '79, '83, '85, '88, '91, '92, '93
Winemaker's food match: Steak, lamb, venison
Retail price: $20
Winemaker: Gavin Berry

RESTRAINED & ELEGANT REDS - full bodied

Plantagenet Shiraz (Mount Barker) preBM

A medium to full bodied, fruit driven wine that typically shows good depth of flavour with some peppery, spicy Shiraz characters and, in certain vintages, some wonderful violet aromas that are typical of the region. Delicious.

Aging potential: 4-12 years
Greatest vintages still drinking well: '80, '82, '83, '86, '90, '91, '94
Recommended food match: Game, steak.
Retail price: $19
Winemaker: Gavin Berry

Technical data: After fermentation the wine is matured in mostly one year old oak casks for 18 months.

Preece Cabernets (Goulburn Valley) V

A pleasing, fruit-driven style, dusty black currant/cassis aromas and flavours are typical of this wine. The palate is quite rich with ample 'sweet' fruit balanced with soft tannins and fresh acid. The soft finish makes this wine approachable now.

Aging potential: This wine is designed to drink well at the time of release however it will hold for up to ten years.
Greatest vintages still drinking well: '89, '92, '93, '94
Winemaker's food match: steak and kidney casserole, rare rump steak, Mungareena cheese.
Retail price: $14
Winemaker: Don Lewis

Technical data: In the vineyard the emphasis is on crop level and minimal irrigation. In the winemaking process a submerged cap (as opposed to floating) is used via a network of timbers. This technique results in a softening of the wine. No maceration on skins is used. Only 5% new oak is used to mature the wine, the balance of the wine spending approximately 14 months in 2-5 year old hogsheads.

*Redbank Sally's Paddock (Pyrenees) BM

A deceptive wine in that its elegance in the mouth in no way foretells the wine's power and longevity. Sally's is typically complex with berry and cassis flavours, some spice characters and in certain years an earthiness in the background. Soft yet assertive tannins are the norm as is good length of flavour.

Aging potential: Good vintages generally peak around 8-10 years of age.
Greatest vintages still drinking well: '82, '84, '86, '88, '90, '91, '92, '93
Retail price: $35
Winemaker: Neil Robb

*Rothbury Reserve Shiraz (Hunter Valley) BM

Soft, perfectly balanced wine of great length and refinement. Red currants, cherries and charry oak characters (more reminiscent of Bordeaux than the Hunter!) are typically complexed by subtle herbal and truffle nuances. A truly astounding red, that ranks amongst Australia's finest Shiraz.

Aging potential: Drinks wonderfully on release, however, those who cellar the Rothbury Reserve for at least ten years will be amply rewarded. I will not be surprised if these wines live and develop favourably for several decades.
Greatest vintages still drinking well: '89, '91, '93
Retail price: $32
Winemaker: Peter Hall

*Saltram Classic Shiraz (SA multi regional blend) V

This label has been inconsistent but the '90 and '92 vintages were wonderful for the price. These wines exhibited smooth, plummy Shiraz flavours, a touch of spice and well integrated, vanillin oak characters.

Aging potential: 5 years
Greatest vintages still drinking well: '90, '92, '94
Retail price: $12
Winemaker: Nigel Dolan

Sandstone Cabernet Sauvignon (Margaret River) preBM

An elegant yet powerful Cabernet which typically exhibits berry fruit characteristics, smoky oak and an earthy complexity. This is definitely a wine that will benefit from time in the cellar.

Aging potential: 5-20 years
Greatest vintages still drinking well: '90, '91, '92, '94
Winemaker's food match: Lamb and other red meats.
Retail price: $20
Winemaker: Jan and mike Davies

Technical data: The grapes are picked at around 13degrees Baume and a relatively warm and fast fermentation follows. The wine stays on skins for around a month before it is pressed. After settling, it is racked into new and one year old oak (a mixture of Nevers and American). After 12-16 months in oak, the wine is filtered and bottled, then rested for at least six months prior to release.

Seppelt Black Label Cabernet Sauvignon (SA multi regional blend) V

A characteristically soft, full flavoured wine exhibiting ripe berry\cassis fruit flavours, a hint of mint and vanillin (oak) in the background, providing extra sweetness and soft tannins.

Aging potential: 3-6 years
Greatest vintages still drinking well: '88, '90, '91
Retail price: $10
Winemaker: Ian McKenzie

Technical data: Sourced from McLaren Vale, Padthaway, Langhorne Creek, and Coonawarra. The wine spends 12 months in French and American oak (generally 1 year old).

*Seppelt Black Label Shiraz (SA & Victoria multi regional blend) V

A rather inconsistent label that has none the less offered tremendous value in its better vintages. Style varies yet it is typically a middleweight that shows good balance between plummy fruit and oak.

Aging potential: 3-5 years
Greatest vintages still drinking well: '87, '88, '89, '90, '92
Retail price: $10
Winemaker: Ian McKenzie

Seppelt Chalambar Shiraz (Victoria multi regional blend) V

A fruit driven style that characteristically shows an impressive depth of Shiraz fruit (berries, mint, pepper) and well integrated oak (spicy, vanilla).

Aging potential: 5-6 years
Greatest vintages still drinking well: '91
Winemaker's food match: Richly sauced pasta, lamb or hearty beef dishes.
Retail price: $14
Winemaker: Ian McKenzie

Technical data: 100% Shiraz (Predominantly Grampians, with fruit also sourced from other Victorian premium regions such as Avoca, Geelong, and the Ovens Valley). Aged for around 15 months in 40% new French oak and 60% 1 year old French oak.

Seppelt Great Western "St Peters" Shiraz (Grampians) BM

This wine demonstrates the affinity between the Great Western region and Shiraz which together produce wines of immense flavour and aging potential. Typically shows good intensity of Shiraz flavours (spicy, berry) firm astringency, and superbly integrated French oak.

Aging potential: 5-10 years+
Greatest vintages still drinking well: '69, '71, '72, '82, '85, '86, '91, '94
Winemaker's food match: cheese, Wimmera rack of lamb
Retail price: $28
Winemaker: Ian McKenzie

Technical data: A single vineyard wine sourced completely from Seppelt' St Peters vineyard. This vineyards 50 year+ old vines are non-irrigated and very low yielding (1.5 t/acre). The wine spends 18 months in new French (Nevers) oak.

*Seville Estate Cabernet Sauvignon (Yarra Valley) preBM

A classic Yarra Cabernet that is typically a mouthful of elegance with lifted berry characters and stylish oak handling.

Aging potential: 5-10 years
Greatest vintages still drinking well: '82, '84, '86, '88, '90, '91, '92, '93, '94
Retail price: $20
Winemaker: Peter McMahon

*Seville Estate Shiraz (Yarra Valley) BM

A liquid argument for more Shiraz to be planted in the Yarra Valley. Vibrant red berry fruits with a streak of pepper/spice are typical of this delicious middleweight.

Aging potential: 2-7 years
Greatest vintages still drinking well: '88, '89, '91, '92 '93, '94
Retail price: $24
Winemaker: Peter McMahon

*Sharefarmers Blend (Naracoorte, bordering Coonawarra) V

One of the few predominantly Malbec blends on the market. It is typically soft with some cassis and berry fruit along with a streak of musk. A pleasant middleweight.

Aging potential: 4-6 years
Greatest vintages still drinking well: '91, '92
Retail price: $14
Winemaker: Brian Croser

*Tyrrell's Old Winery Cabernet Merlot (Coonawarra/McLaren Vale) V

This has developed into one of the best value middle-weight reds on the market, typically exhibiting plummy, sweet Cabernet fruit and sometimes a delicious gamy, earthy characters. The '94 with its pristine 'Ribena' aromas and flavours was one of the best buys I'd seen for quite a while.

Aging potential: Delicious when young, this early drinking style will develop added complexity with 2-5 years in the cellar.
Greatest vintages still drinking well: '91, '92, '93, '94
Retail Price: $12
Winemaker: Andrew Spinnaze

Vasse Felix Cabernet Sauvignon (Margaret River) preBM

Typically exhibits substantial depth of flavour (mulberry, leafy, dusty, other red berries) with a soft and well balanced mouthfeel. Oak is clearly evident, without ever dominating, giving the wine a cedar oil character and a soft roundness. Fine, furry tannins are typical on the finish. Very stylish drinking.

Aging potential: 10-15+ years. A '78 opened recently drank beautifully.
Greatest vintages still drinking well: '76, '77, '78, '85, '91, '90
Winemaker's food match: Rich foods such as red meats, pizza, pasta, cheese
Retail price: $25
Winemaker: Clive Otto

Technical data: Comes from the oldest vines in the Margaret River.

*Vasse Felix Shiraz (Margaret River) BM

This wine typically exhibits the velvety mouthfeel that one expects of this variety in the Margaret River, along with an excellent depth of concentrated fruit characteristics (blackberry/plum) intermingled with rich, yet balanced, oak characteristics of vanilla and spice. A wonderfully soft yet richly flavoured palate are the norm here.

Aging potential: 3-8 years
Greatest vintages still drinking well: '88, '90, '91, '93
Retail price: $25 (Ex Winery)
Winemaker: Clive Otto

Technical data: 20% of the wine is barrel fermented in new American oak and the wine spends around twelve months in 80% American and 20% new French oak.

Virgin Hills (Macedon) BM

Tremendously stylish wine, perfectly balanced on release, characteristically exhibiting a peppery/spicy bouquet and berry\ blackcurrant flavour crafted into a mouthfeel that is liquid elegance. In good vintages, this is about as refined as it gets.

Aging potential: 5-8 years
Greatest vintages still drinking well: '74, '79, '80, '82, '85, '88, '92
Winemaker's food match: Lighter red meats, mature cheeses.
Retail price: $30
Winemaker: Mark Sheppard

Technical data: Virgin Hills is made from 100% estate grown grapes and is matured in 40% new French oak (Allier/Troncais). No sulphur (So2, preservative 220) is added in the winemaking process.

Wynns Coonawarra Hermitage (Coonawarra) V

A soft, richly flavoured Shiraz that typically shows, in successful vintages, the flavours of plums, mulberry and raspberry, sweet vanillin oak characteristics, and a spiciness that varies from vintage to vintage (the cooler the year, the more spicy the wine).

Aging potential: Will generally peak between 4-10 years although great vintages have the capacity to live for several decades.
Greatest vintages still drinking well: '53, '54, '55, '62, '66, '76, (only bottles cellared in ideal conditions) and '82, '86, '90, '93
Recommended food match: Red meats and soft cheeses. Matches extremely well with grilled meats.
Retail price: $12
Winemaker: Peter Douglas

RESTRAINED & ELEGANT REDS - full bodied

Yeringberg "Yeringberg" (Formerly Cabernet) (Yarra Valley) BM

Typically a refined style of wine with soft tannins, clean acidity and intense yet subtle fruit flavours. Spicy oak characters are expected and, sometimes, a hint of grassiness. Always very classy.

Aging potential: Will improve with age (12-18 years).
Greatest vintages still drinking well: '75, '76, '77, '79, '80, '81, '86, '88, '90, '91, '94
Winemaker's food match: Roast lamb
Retail price: $27
Winemaker: Guill De Pury

Technical data: The wine is blended from Cabernet Sauvignon, Cabernet Franc, Merlot grapes that are harvested as ripe as possible to maximise fruit flavour.. The wine is matured in French oak barrels, one third of which are new (and therefore impart more oak character to the wine).

Other Recommended Producers: Calais, De Bortoli Yarra Valley, Devil's Lair, Diamond Valley, Dromana Estate, Geoff Weaver Stafford Ridge, Joseph Moda Amerone and Double Pruned Cabernet Sauvignon, McWilliams ('Single Vineyard', 'O'Shea', 'Special Release'), Mildara, Petersons, Rothbury Reserve Shiraz, Saddler's Creek, St Huberts, Tim Knappstein "The Franc", Yarra Burn, amongst others

PINOT NOIR

Although most of these Pinots are substantially lighter in body than the Cabernet Sauvignons and Shiraz wines listed above, they are none the less fleshy wines with good intensity of flavour and as such I consider it inaccurate to describe them as 'light reds'. It is with this logic that I have placed them under their own heading.

In its short history, Australian Pinot Noir has been often malined for being too light and thinly flavoured. In the not so distant past this criticism may have been justified, however, the quality of these wines has improved dramatically over the last five years and they now rank amongst our most elegant and delicious reds. Pinot Noir is costly to produce and this outlay is reflected in the retail price. Are the benchmark examples worth the thirty odd dollars? Compared to the reds of Burgundy, France (the region that produces the greatest Pinot Noirs) the best Australian Pinots not only justify their price but represent unequivocal bargains. Australian Pinots are generally not worth aging more than five years although there are exceptions (see winemakers recommendations).

Sorrenburg Gamay has also been included below. Although this wine has only a small percentage of Pinot Noir, it is similar in weight to many of the wines listed here.

LEGEND OF SYMBOLS

"**BM**" - stands for bench-mark. Wines titles that are followed by this symbol are wines to measure others by.

"**preBM**" - indicates a wine that has shown itself capable of achieving a BM standard however the 'label' lacks either a long enough history of vintages or perhaps the consistency to be titled as such.

"**V**" - stands for Value. These wines represent very good examples of their region and/or wine style, and are relatively inexpensive (at least under $20).

"*****" - the author has compiled this wine description with little if any feed-back from the producer.

Ashton Hills Pinot Noir (Piccadilly Valley, Adelaide Hills) preBM

Ashton Pinot Noir is a light to medium bodied dry red with plenty of classic Pinot Noir flavours (strawberry/cherry) and subtle, spicy oak. Because of Ashton Hills' cool climate vineyards and the youthfulness of its vines there has been a significant variation in style between vintages. Such variation will continue for some time and may even increase as more of Ashton Hill's 17 Pinot Noir clones come into bearing. Quality has improved with each vintage and the '93 was wonderful drinking. I'm backing this wine to establish itself as worthy of a BM rating over the next few years.

Aging potential: Early vintages: 3-5years. From 1993: 5-10 years
Greatest vintages: '88, '91, '93, '94
Winemaker's food match: Extremely adaptable food wine which only gets lost with powerfully flavoured dishes such as barbequed meat. Otherwise it is fine, even with fish.
Retail price: $21
Winemaker: Stephen George

Technical data: The vineyards experience cold wet winters, relatively cool summers and quite high humidity throughout the year. This climate is very similar to Burgundy and contributes to the 'correct' Pinot Noir flavours in the wine. The vineyard is sloped gently to the south and consists of well drained sandy loam over friable sandstone. Bunch thinning and the use of a Scott-Henry trellis system (very high but narrow) in the vineyard ensures fruit ripeness by allowing good sunlight penetration. The wine undergoes a hot fermentation, with some whole bunches and stalks plus a period of maceration of skins. This gives the wine complex flavours that would otherwise be lacking. The wine spends about a year in oak before bottling but most of the oak is not new.

*Bannockburn Pinot Noir (Geelong) BM

One of Australia's finest and most consistent Pinot Noirs that keeps on getting better and better. It typically exhibits intense, ripe, mouthfilling Pinot Noir fruit without any cost to the wine's elegance, softness and sappy length. Spicy oak is also typical along with some fine tannins on the finish.

Aging potential: 4 - 10 years
Greatest vintages still drinking well: '86, '88, '89, '90, '91, '92, '94
Retail price: $33
Winemaker: Gary Farr

*Coldstream Hills "Reserve" Pinot Noir (Yarra Valley) BM

Typically exhibits strawberry\cherry flavours, first class toasty, spicy oak and a wonderful sappy finish.

Aging potential: 3-8 years
Greatest vintages: '88, '90, '91, '92, '94
Retail price: $30
Winemaker: James Halliday and Phillip Dowell

Delamere Pinot Noir (Pipers Brook) preBM

A wine that keeps improving with each vintage - the '93 is the best to date. Pipers Brook Pinot is for lovers of the more delicate style of Pinot. This example is typically light in structure yet with good depth of fruit and a highly aromatic bouquet of strawberries and spice.

Aging potential: 4-10 years
Greatest vintages: '88, '90, '91, '93
Winemaker's food match: Liver dishes such as pate or terrine and soft cheeses.
Retail price: $22
Winemaker: Richard H Richardson

*Diamond Valley Blue label Pinot Noir (Yarra Valley) V

Typically a lovely middleweight with a soft, juicy palate that is full of flavour and exhibits a whisper of spicy oak.

Aging potential: 2-4 years
Greatest vintages: '90, '91, '92, '93
Retail price: $17
Winemaker: David Lance

*Diamond Valley Estate 'White label' Pinot Noir (Yarra Valley) BM

Great depth and complexity of flavour are two of this wines highlights. Rich dark cherry\strawberry fruit characteristics, high quality oak, fine tannins, and a long sappy finish are all typical of this wine. So are flavours that defy words and linger eternally on the breath like the whispers of angels.

Aging potential: 3-8 years
Greatest vintages: '86, '88, '90, '91, '92, '93, '94
Retail price: $33
Winemaker: David Lance

Hainault "Reserve" Pinot Noir (Perth Hills) preBM

A delicious medium bodied and complex wine with a perfumed nose of crushed violets and reseda and an intriguing silken palate redolent of black truffles, forest floor, cedar and fine leather. Typically exhibits a smooth, rich and long palate.

Aging potential: Expected to be around 8-12 years
Greatest vintages still drinking well: '89, '90, '92, '94
Recommended food match: Game or venison especially with truffles
Retail price: $28
Winemaker: Peter Fimmel

Technical data: Perth Hills soils and elevation above sea level impart a firm structure when young which gradually opens up and develops further complexity with cellaring. The wine undergoes prolonged fermentation of uncrushed grapes followed by mixed new and old French oak maturation.

Giaconda Pinot Noir (Beechworth) BM

This wine typically exhibits a complex "Burgundian" nose of strawberries, plums, cherries and some gamy characteristics lurking in the background waiting to emerge with bottle age. The palate has good depth of flavour, a silky structure, and fine tannins.

Aging potential: 5 years
Greatest vintages still drinking well: '88, '89, '92
Recommended food match: Best with game dishes
Retail price: $27
Winemaker: Rick Kinzbrunner

Technical data: Traditional Burgundian winemaking techniques are used including the use of 50% new French oak of the highest quality. The wine is matured in barrel for about 18 months and bottled without filtration.

*Lenswood Vineyards Pinot Noir (Adelaide Hills) preBM

More potential than Tony Blair, this wine has, in three short vintages, stated its intention to become one of Australia's finest expressions of the Pinot Noir grape. The '93 vintage, which is clearly the finest release so far, is packed with marinated cherry fruit and spicy oak, all within as soft and refined a structure as one could imagine. And the '94, although less powerful, is not far behind.

Aging potential: Should benefit from around 3-5 years in the bottle.
Greatest vintages still drinking well: '93, '94
Retail price: $30
Winemaker: Tim Knappstein

Main Ridge Pinot Noir (Mornington Peninsula) BM

One of the riper Pinots from the Mornington Peninsula this wine typically exhibits spicy, sweet fruit characteristics (dark cherry/plum), warm alcohol, and a velvety mouth-feel.

Aging potential: Drinks well from 3 years of age although good vintages will keep for at least 10 years.
Greatest vintages still drinking well: '88, '91, '92, '93, '94
Recommended food match: Rich meat/game dishes
Retail price: $26
Winemaker: Nat White

Technical data: The Main Ridge vineyards, due to crop reduction, no irrigation, and the peninsula's cool climate, are very low yielding (1.5 tonnes/acre), and this results in intensely flavoured grapes. Scott Henry trellising has been used to maximise ripeness. The wine is fermented in open vats with some whole bunches and frequent cap plunging by foot. The wine remains on skins for 18 days after which it is matured in French oak barriques.

*Montara Pinot Noir (Grampians) preBM

One of Australia's best value Pinots. Typically Australian in style it exhibits intense, mouthfilling fruit characters of plums, and black cherries along with a spiciness, soft tannins and a delicious savoury finish. It is bigger and richer than most Pinots and will therefore hold its own against richer foods.

Aging potential: 5-10 years
Greatest vintages still drinking well: '86, '88, '92, '93, '94
Retail price: $18
Winemaker: Mike McRae

Moorooduc Estate Pinot Noir (Mornington Peninsula) preBM

This wine varies according to vintage from a lightly coloured but intensely fragrant wine with a sweet middle palate and great length, to a wine with a lot of colour and structure. Sweet plum, cherry aromas and flavours become modified with bottle age by earthy, sappy and fungal (mushroom, truffle) secondary characters.

Aging potential: This will vary with different vintages but all will show the benefits of 3-5 years of aging. Some of the bigger wines should last a lot longer than that.
Greatest vintages still drinking well: '91, '92, '93, '94
Winemaker's food match: Game dishes (such as stuffed quail) or mushrooms go particularly well with these wines. They can also so compliment many Asian dishes.
Retail price: $23
Winemaker: Richard McIntyre

Technical data: This is an estate grown wine made from three clones of Pinot Noir vines. The wine is fermented in open stainless steel fermenters with a percentage of whole bunches. Relatively hot fermentation temperatures are sought and up to three weeks skin contact is used before pressing. A small proportion of wine in recent years has finished its fermentation in the barrel and all wine spends twelve months in French oak.

Mountadam Pinot Noir (Adelaide Hills) preBM

Typically a rich, complex style of Pinot Noir that exhibits an enticing nose of dark cherries and strawberries and a full rounded palate with firm yet fine tannins.

Aging potential: 4-10 years
Greatest vintages: '84, '88, '91, '93
Winemaker's food match: This wine is very good with quail, pigeon or duck.
Retail price: $25
Winemaker : Adam Wynn

Technical data: Winemaker Adam Wynn is obsessed with complexity of flavour. To achieve these ends he utilises the 9 clones of Pinot Noir in his low yielding vineyards by making separate parcels of wines in different ways before blending them into the final wine. French oak (Troncais) is used.

*Mount Mary Pinot Noir (Yarra Valley) BM

One of Australia's most refined and beautifully balanced Pinot Noirs. Great depth of soft, supple Pinot fruit, length of flavour and longevity are its trademarks.

Aging potential: 6-15 yrs
Greatest vintages still drinking well: '82, '86, '88, '89, '90, '91, '92
Retail price: $50
Winemaker : John Middleton

Nicholson River Pinot Noir (Gippsland) preBM

One of the most powerful Pinots on the market this wine typically exhibits gamy, spicy-perfumed aromas and enormous weight of flavour on the palate. This is an intense "Australian style" Pinot that is richly flavoured and complex, soft yet powerful, and generally in need of 4-5 years bottle age.

Aging potential: 5-10 years
Greatest vintages still drinking well: With each vintage the quality of wine improves.
Recommended food match: Game such as venison, duck or rabbit etc.
Retail price: Generally not available through retail outlets. Mostly sold at cellar door for $25.
Winemaker: Ken Eckersley

Technical data: Nicholson River vineyards are very low yielding (1 ton/acre) which partially explains the intensity of flavour in the wine. It is matured in oak for 1.5-2yrs prior to bottling.

*Scotchmans Hill Pinot Noir (Geelong) preBM

An instant cult winery amongst Victorian and New South Welsh consumers, Scotchmans Hill produces richly flavoured, perfumed Pinot Noir with juicy fruit and spicy oak characters. Recent vintages have clearly been of BM quality and future consistency will merit such a rating.

Aging potential: 5-10 years
Greatest vintages still drinking well: Whilst the last three vintages, '92-'94 have been my favourites, all are drinking well.
Retail price: $25
Winemaker: Robin Brockett

Sorrenberg Gamay (Beechworth) preBM

A delicious middleweight that winemaker Barry Morey describes as a cross between the heavier Beaujolais styles and the wines of the Rhone. It typically exhibits red fruits and spice characters, zesty acidity and subtle tannins on the finish. It shows full ripeness without any jamminess and has the balanced acid, and complexity to go with a wide range of foods. May earn a BM rating with a few more vintages.

Aging potential: 3-8 years
Greatest vintages still drinking well: '93, '94
Winemaker's food match: Antipasto, pasta, soups (spicy)
Retail price: $19
Winemaker: Barry Morey

Technical data: The vineyard is at 550m altitude and is of granitic soils. This wine is a blend of 90% Gamay, 10% Pinot of which 30%-40% is treated with new French (Burgundian) oak. The wine is left on its lees for 8 months. 30% whole bunches are used in the fermentation which is carried out to completion on skins, then left on skins for a further 7-10 days. All these techniques add to the overall weight and complexity of the wine.

*Stoniers Reserve Pinot Noir (Mornington Peninsula) BM

A soft and elegant wine that typically exhibits an amalgam of classic Pinot Noir aromas and flavours. Intense, ripe fruit characters, a balance of all components and a lingering finish are what we have come to expect of this wine.

Aging potential: An early drinking style however better vintages will repay up to 5 years of cellaring.
Greatest vintages still drinking well: '90, '91, '91, '92, '94
Retail price: $25
Winemaker: Tod Dexter

*Wignalls Pinot Noir (Albany, Lower Great Southern) preBM

This wine has caused something of a sensation in the West, winning many awards and being hailed by many as WA's greatest Pinot. It is typically elegant in the mouth with cherry/berry flavours and a gamy complexity. In 1993 Wignalls produced a 'Reserve' Pinot Noir that was nothing short of sublime. Should they continue doing so, the wine would most surely warrant a BM listing in this guide.

Aging potential: At this stage, this appears to be an early drinking wine that will only benefit, if at all, from 2-4 years in the bottle.
Greatest vintages still drinking well: '92, '93, '94
Retail price: $25
Winemaker: John Wade

Yeringberg Pinot Noir (Yarra Valley) BM

An elegant yet full flavoured red that typically exhibits ripe fruit flavours (strawberry\cherry\spice), velvety mouth feel, and supportive oak in the background (smoky). A complex Pinot with a pleasing sappiness on the finish.

Aging potential: Yeringberg Pinot benefits greatly from a few years bottle aging. It will continue to improve for up to 10 years or more. Years with ripe fruit and high alcohol mature longer. '81 is now in its prime, whilst '86 is also drinking very well.
Greatest vintages still drinking well: '80, '81, '83, '86, '89, '90, '91, '92 (Vintages pre-1980 should be consumed soon).
Winemaker's food match: duck, beef, venison
Retail price: $23
Winemaker: Guill De Pury

Technical data: 100% Pinot Noir from low yielding vineyards. The wine is matured in French oak barrels of which about 1/4 are new each year. The grapes as picked as ripe as possible and fermentation occurs at relatively warm temperatures.

*Yarra Yering Pinot Noir (Yarra Valley) BM

One of Australia's bigger, richer styles of Pinot yet despite this it sacrifices no refinement in the mouth. This wine typically exhibits ripe Pinot flavours in the plum\strawberry spectrum along with spicy, chocolaty oak characteristics and soft but assertive tannins.

Aging potential: One of the better cellaring styles this wine will benefit from 4-8 years of cellaring and will often live and develop longer.
Greatest vintages still drinking well: '86, '87, '90, '91, '92.
Retail price: $55
Winemaker: Bailey Carrodus

Other Recommended Producers: Grosset, Lillydale, Massoni, Salitage, Smithbrook, Springvale, Wantirna, amongst others

LIGHT REDS AND ROSÉ

I find it bewildering that despite our warm to sizzling climate, so few of these thirst quenching wines are produced in Australia. Good rosés are delicious chilled, as are light reds (although the latter can also be served at room temperature). They can be served with a wide variety of food (especially Asian or Italian dishes) and one needs no better reason than a parched throat to pull the cork. In spite of their attributes, there are so few of these wines produced, and in such limited quantities, that I am loathe to announce the names of these treasures to the world.

LEGEND OF SYMBOLS

"**BM**" - stands for bench-mark. Wines titles that are followed by this symbol are wines to measure others by.

"**preBM**" - indicates a wine that has shown itself capable of achieving a BM standard however the 'label' lacks either a long enough history of vintages or perhaps the consistency to be titled as such.

"**V**" - stands for Value. These wines represent very good examples of their region and/or wine style, and are relatively inexpensive (at least under $20).

"*" - the author has compiled this wine description with little if any feed-back from the producer.

*Bannockburn Saignee (Geelong) BM

The sole benchmark wine in this listing, Bannockburn Saignee is typically a wickedly delicious wine made from the free-run juice of Pinot Noir. It is soft and dry, with juicy strawberry flavours, a hint of spiciness, and cleansing acidity on the finish.

Aging potential: A drink-now style that will not benefit from further cellaring.
Retail price: $18
Winemaker: Garry Farr

*Brown Brothers Tarrango (Nth Eastern Victoria) V

A deliciously refreshing light red that is typically packed with raspberry\strawberry fruit and zesty acid.

Aging potential: A drink-now style that will not benefit from further cellaring.
Retail price: $10
Winemaker: Roland Wahlquist

*Charles Melton Rosé of Virginia (Barossa Valley) V

A full flavoured rosé that typically exhibits the aromas and flavours of red berries, a hint of sweetness, and good acidity on the finish.

Aging potential: A drink-now style that will not benefit from further cellaring.
Retail price: $10
Winemaker: Charles Melton

Houghton Cabernet Rosé (Swan Valley) V

A light and crisp wine that typically exhibits the flavours of fresh berries along with a pleasant grassy streak and a soft finish.

Aging potential: This wine does not benefit from age and is therefore best drunk within twelve months of vintage.
Winemaker's food match: Cold or lightly flavoured meats and spicy foods.
Retail price: $12
Winemaker: Paul Lapsley

Technical data: The most successful Rosé at Australian wine shows post 1980. Made from early picked Cabernet Sauvignon sourced from Houghton's Moondah Brook (Upper Swan Valley) vineyards. The grapes are night harvested and crushed early in the morning. The juice is fermented on the skins, until the wine has picked up a light crimson colour, at which point the wine is drained of its skins and fermentation is completed in the same manner as a white wine. The resulting wine is the bottled ASAP to maximise freshness.

*Rockford Alicante Bouschet Rosé (Barossa Valley) preBM

Delicious dry, light red with enough fruit flavour (spiced cherry, strawberry) to go with the spiciest of food. Very morish.

Aging potential: A drink-now style that will not benefit from further cellaring.
Retail price: $14
Winemaker: Robert O'Callaghan

*Schinus Rosé (Yarra Valley + other Victorian regions) V

Made from the free run juice of Pinot Noir and Cabernet Sauvignon grapes this wine typically exhibits a zesty, crisp palate laden with berry flavours.

Aging potential: A drink-now style that will not benefit from further cellaring.
Retail price: $13
Winemaker: Garry Crittenden

Taltarni Pyrenees (Pyrenees) V

Taltarni Rosé des Pyrenees (Pyrenees) V

This wine is typically pale salmon in colour with a fresh spicy aroma, fruity palate, and a crisp dry finish.

Aging potential: This style of wine does not benefit from aging. Drink whilst young and fresh.
Winemaker's food match: Japanese, Chinese, or a perfect picnic wine
Retail price: $12
Winemaker: Dominique Portet and Greg Gallagher

Technical data: Made from 100% Malbec grapes, the wine receives its colour by being left on the grapes red skins (maceration) for a short period of time.

Other Recommended Producers: All Saints Aleatico, Ninth Island, amongst others

CRISP & DRY WHITES

These wines show an austerity of flavour in their youth, along with crisp acid and a streak of herbaceousness that makes them amongst the most refreshing of beverages. Young, unwooded Semillon from the Margaret River region of WA and the lower Hunter valley of NSW are good examples. Although many understandably prefer to wait for Hunter Semillon to achieve more richness and complexity with bottle age I am of the opinion that their youthful elegance is underappreciated.

LEGEND OF SYMBOLS

"BM" - stands for bench-mark. Wines titles that are followed by this symbol are wines to measure others by.

"preBM" - indicates a wine that has shown itself capable of producing wines of a BM standard however the 'label' lacks either a long enough history of vintages or perhaps the consistency to be titled as such.

"V" - stands for Value. These wines represent very good examples of their region and/or wine style, and are relatively inexpensive (at least under $20).

"*" - the author has compiled this wine description with little if any feed-back from the producer.

Briar Ridge Semillon (Lower Hunter) preBM

Generally a light straw coloured wine with fresh, citrus-like aroma and a soft easy-to-drink palate. This full flavoured Semillon typically finishes with good crisp acidity and a lasting flavour. A rich honeyed character will develop with bottle age.

Aging potential: 3-4 yrs
Greatest vintages still drinking well: '91, '93
Winemaker's food match: seafood, veal, chicken all go well with this wine.
Retail price: $16
Winemaker: Kees Van de Scheur 1988-'93, Pip Treadwell '94, Neil McGuigan '95

Technical data: The wine is bottled early to retain a fresh fruity flavours. No oak maturation is given to the wine.

Briar Ridge Stockhausen Semillon (Lower Hunter) BM

Typically a traditional Hunter Semillon with good varietal characteristics, such as citrus (lime/lemon) aromas and flavours. A dry yet soft Semillon which typically exhibits good depth of flavour and a clean crisp finish which tends to fill out with honeyed/toasty flavours as the wine ages. The '91 vintage of this wine was sublime.

Aging potential: 5 years, longer in some cases and considerably longer in great vintages such as the '91.
Greatest vintages still drinking well: '91, '92, '94
Winemaker's food match: As a young wine it is a good accompaniment for oysters and any seafood. As a mature wine it will compliment chicken or veal in a creamy sauce
Retail price: $20
Winemaker: Karl Stockhausen

*Brokenwood Semillon (Lower Hunter) BM

Typically a crisp, austere wine with gooseberry and grassy characters and citrussy acid. In some years a floral/passionfruit character is also evident. Delicious.

Aging potential: 4-7 years
Greatest vintages still drinking well: '85, '91, '92, '94
Retail price: $20
Winemaker: Iain Riggs

Chateau Tahbilk Marsanne (Goulburn Valley) preBM

A lighter bodied, crisp wine when young, Tahbilk Marsanne traditionally exhibits aromas in the lemon, honey and peach spectrums. The palate typically has lemon and peach fruit flavours with chalky acidity balancing the wine and standing it in good stead for years to come. With bottle age the wine gains complexity, richness and the "honeysuckle" fragrance traditionally associated with the Marsanne grape.

Aging potential: Average years: 3-4, Good years: 5-6 years, Great years: 7-10
Greatest vintages still drinking well: '80, '82, '89, '92, '94
Winemaker's food match: Asian, especially Chinese cooking, white meats, pasta, seafood, salads
Retail price: $11
Winemaker: Alister Purbrick

Technical data: The wine is made utilising cold fermentation techniques and total exclusion of oxygen which maximises flavour and freshness. The juice is fermented in stainless steel tanks. On completion of fermentation it is stabilised and filtered prior to bottling. Marsanne is not matured in oak and is a fruit driven style.

*Lenswood Vineyards Sauvignon Blanc (Adelaide Hills) preBM

The early vintages of this wine have signalled a departure from the typical style of Australian Sauvignon. It has thus far exhibited varietal characteristics of asparagus, gooseberry and subtle stone fruits with a delicacy and balance that many of these wines lack.

Aging potential: Too early to tell, however, it does appear to have the structure to benefit from a few years in bottle.
Greatest vintages still drinking well: '93, '94
Retail price: $20
Winemaker: Tim Knappstein

Lindemans Hunter River Semillon (Lower Hunter) preBM

Typically a fresh grassy, citrus flavoured wine with a medium bodied palate finely balanced by refreshing, crisp acidity.

Aging potential: In standard vintages 3-5 years, in excellent vintages, 8-10 years
Greatest vintages still drinking well: '70, '87, '91, '94
Winemaker's food match: Chicken, seafood
Retail price: $14
Winemaker: Patrick Auld

McWilliams "Elizabeth" Semillon (Lower Hunter) preBM

A wonderful and accessibly priced example of aged Hunter Semillon. On release, usually at around six years of age, this wine typically exhibits the complex aromas of buttered toast and honey. The palate is richly flavoured yet crisp and dry, with nutty, honeyed characters and soft acidity on the finish. Perhaps the greatest value white wine in Australia today.

Aging potential: 8-20 years
Greatest vintages still drinking well: '75, '79, '81, '82, '86, '87, '89, '91, '92, '93, '94
Winemaker's food match: As for 'Lovedale'
Retail price: $13
Winemaker: Phillip Ryan

Technical data: See 'Lovedale' listing next page

McWilliams "Lovedale" Semillon (Lower Hunter) BM

This wine is released with considerable bottle age (at the time of writing, the '86 vintage has only recently become available) which makes it an ideal introduction to mature Hunter Semillon. In its youth the wine typically exhibits aromas in the floral/lemon spectrum or sometimes more grassy and herbaceous characters depending on which part of the vineyard it was sourced. The palate is fresh, spicy and citrus-like and finishes dry with well balanced, crisp acidity. As the wine matures in bottle, the aromas becomes more complex with marked toasty, even butterscotch-like characters. The palate becomes richly flavoured with nutty and honeyed characters. Low in acid, soft, rich and intensely flavoured, this is a Hunter Semillon of the highest quality

Aging potential: 8-20 years
Greatest vintages still drinking well: '75, '79, '84, '86, '87
Winemaker's food match: Any seafood dishes, particularly crustaceans, salads, white meats, lighter flavoured pasta dishes
Retail price: $30
Winemaker: Phillip Ryan

Technical data: Lovedale Semillon is produced from the Lovedale Vineyard situated in the basin of the Lower Hunter valley in Pokolbin. Here the soils are quite light in texture, sandy marine shales and clays that produce a lighter more restrained style of Semillon which matures at a slower rate. This wine undergoes no oak treatment. It is bottled early, within a few weeks after fermentation, this being important to lock in the spicy fresh fruit characters of young Semillon and to assist in future bottle ageing and development. In the hotter, drier vintages the honeyed, nutty flavours and aromas will develop more quickly while in the cooler, wetter years the wines take longer to develop.

*Moss Wood Margaret River Semillon (Unwooded) BM

A fine, zesty Semillon that typically exhibits gooseberry and lemon-like fruit along with a hint of grass and vibrant yet soft acidity

Aging potential: 4-12 years
Greatest vintages: '85, '87, '90, '92, '93 '95
Retail price: $20
Winemaker: Keith Mugford

*Mount Mary "Triolet" (Yarra Valley) BM

Typically a soft, dry wine that exhibits tropical fruit characters with a streak of herbaceousness. Relatively high alcohol tends to give the wine a gentle sweetness on the finish. One of the few in this category that will benefit from some bottle age.

Aging potential: 4-8 years
Greatest vintages still drinking well: '89, '90, '91,'92, '93
Retail price: $40
Winemaker: John Middleton

Plantagenet "Omrah" (Mount Barker) preBM

A clean crisp wine typically exhibiting pristine Chardonnay fruit flavours of melon and ripe peaches.

Aging potential: 2-3 years
Greatest vintages still drinking well: '92, '94
Winemaker's food match: oysters and other seafood, pasta, vegetarian
Retail price: $15
Winemaker: Gavin Berry

*Rothbury Hunter Semillon (Lower Hunter) BM

Typically a crisp citrussy wine packed with the aromas of straw, grass, and gooseberry balanced by lively acidity. Although this is a wonderfully zesty wine when young it really needs time in the cellar to show its mettle.

Aging potential: 6-12 years
Greatest vintages still drinking well: '84, '86, '89, '91, '92, '94
Retail price: $14
Winemaker: Peter Hall

*Tyrrell's Lost Block Semillon (Lower Hunter) V

A richer, riper style of Hunter Semillon packed with citrus and straw characters and a soft, rounded mouthfeel. Despite being bigger and juicier than one would normally expect from Lower Hunter Semillon, it is none the less a crisp and refreshing wine that sits well in this category.

Aging potential: 2-5 years
Greatest vintages still drinking well: '93, '94
Retail price: $17
Winemaker: Andrew Spinnaze

*Tyrrell's Vat 1 Semillon (confusingly labelled as "Riesling") BM

Few labels can challenge Vat 1 in both consistency and quality as the finest example of Hunter Semillon over the last ten years. Typically a tight, herbaceous wine in its youth, it is often low in alcohol (a good sign in these wines) yet rounded with straw and lemony characters and crisp acid on the finish. Tends to hold its structure with age so that although it gains the 'buttered toast' typical of these wines, it rarely becomes fat or oily in texture.

Aging potential: 6-15 years
Greatest vintages still drinking well: '80, '83, '84, '85, '86, '87, '88, '89, '91, '92, '93, '94
Retail price: $25
Winemaker: Andrew Spinnaze

Yeringberg "Yeringberg" (Yarra Valley) [formerly Marsanne] preBM

Striking, austere dry white with some floral and honey hints. When the wine is young it is subtly flavoured and is therefore best served cool rather than chilled. With age (5 years or more) the flavours broaden and the wine shows a rich honeyed character and, sometimes, a distinct earthy complexity.

Aging potential: After 5 or 6 years bottle age the wine has generally hit its peak however it will hold and continue to evolve for many years afterwards.
Greatest vintages still drinking well: '86, '87, '88, '93, '94
Winemaker's food match: Fresh seafood, yabbies, crabs
Retail price: $23
Winemaker: Guill De Pury

Technical data: The wine is a blend of Marsanne (richer flavour) and Roussanne (floral character and acidity); the same varieties that are used to make the white wines of France's Rhone Valley. The wine is matured for six months in old French oak barrels prior to bottling but oak flavour is not an important part of this wine.

Other Recommended producers: Allanmere, Hungerford Hill ("Young Semillon" & ("Tumbarumba Sauvignon Blanc"), Reynolds Semillon, Petersons Semillon, amongst others

DRY RIESLINGS - A CLASS OF THEIR OWN

Riesling, sometimes incorrectly labelled "Rhine" Riesling, is perhaps our most misunderstood wine style. I believe this is mostly due to those partially sweet 4 litre cask wines, scandalously labelled 'Riesling' (scandalously because they are rarely made from Riesling grapes) that often rely more on residual sugar than anything else for their flavour. Also, Riesling is an aromatic grape variety and its heady bouquet along with weight of fruit flavour can give a false impression of sweetness, as can the viscous mouth feel the wine develops with age.

It is disappointing how many people believe that Riesling is a medium-sweet wine. It can, and is, made into a wonderful dessert style, but the wine in the tall, long-necked bottle is, with the exception of certain cheaper wines, always dry. The best examples can be amongst our most delicious and interesting white wines, and many will live and improve for ten to twenty years. With such bottle age these wines will add toasty and intense lime flavours to the citrus/floral zestiness of their youth. (see winemakers' recommendations for aging potential).

These unwooded whites deserve a listing of their own as they defy grouping with any other Australian white. While they are aromatic they have the structure and longevity that other Australian aromatics lack. While they are powerful and rich in flavour they are none the less crisp & dry. They go well with a wide variety of food, or drink wonderfully on their own. Despite growing recognition of the quality of these wines amongst the public, and the subsequent price rises, Riesling remains one of Australia's least expensive great wines.

LEGEND OF SYMBOLS

"**BM**" - stands for bench-mark. Wines titles that are followed by this symbol are wines to measure others by.

"**preBM**" - indicates a wine that has shown itself capable of producing wines of a BM standard however the 'label' lacks either a long enough history of vintages or perhaps the consistency to be titled as such.

"**V**" - stands for Value. These wines represent very good examples of their region and/or wine style, and are relatively inexpensive (at least under $20).

"*****" - the author has compiled this wine description with little if any feed-back from the producer.

Capel Vale Riesling (Mount Barker/Capel) preBM

A distinctive Riesling whose recent vintages have seen a return to the form of the magnificent '86 vintage. Floral, citrus aromas are common here as is a soft, rounded palate with tropical and passionfruit flavours, zesty acid and a hint of sweetness on the finish.

Aging potential: 3-8 years
Greatest vintages still drinking well: ' 86, '88, '90, '91, '92, '93, '95
Retail price: $15
Winemaker: Rob Bowen

*Crawford River Riesling (Western District, Vic) BM

Typically a crisp, light Riesling that is wonderfully perfumed, with floral, passionfruit and lime characters, leading to a long, dry palate. A perfect aperitif or seafood wine.

Aging potential: 3-8 years
Greatest vintages still drinking well: '86, '88, '90, '91, '92, '93
Retail price: $17
Winemaker: John Thomson

*Delatite Riesling (Mansfield) BM

A fresh, vibrant Riesling with crisp acid, intense, limey fruit and a lingering, bone dry finish. This is a wonderful wine without even a hint of the sugary fruitiness that many drinkers mistakenly associate with Riesling.

Aging potential: 3-8 years
Greatest vintages still drinking well: '86, '87, '90, '91, '92, '93, '95
Retail price: $16
Winemaker: Ros Ritchie

*Goundrey Reserve Riesling (Mount Barker) preBM

Typically a zesty Riesling with citrus, white peach and passionfruit characters along with vibrant acidity.

Aging potential: 3-6 years
Greatest vintages still drinking well: '88, '90, '91, '92, '93, '94, '95
Retail price: $15
Winemaker: Brendan Smith

Grosset Watervale Riesling (Watervale, Clare Valley) preBM

A fuller fruitier style than the Polish Hill release from this producer. It is a classic example of the richly flavoured, yet dry Riesling for which the Clare Valley is renown.

Aging potential: 6-10 years
Greatest vintages still drinking well: '82, '86, '87, '90, '94, '95
Retail price: $14
Winemaker: Jeffrey Grosset

Technical data: The vineyard is a classic example of the best in the district, planted in red loam over limestone.

Grosset Polish Hill Riesling (Polish Hill, Clare Valley) BM

Crisp, clean, intense flavours in the citrus spectrum with zesty acidity completing the picture. A bone dry Riesling of great finesse and elegance.

Aging potential: 7-15 years
Greatest vintages still drinking well: '82, '86, '87, '90, '94, '95
Winemaker's food match: Goes well with a wide variety of foods but whiting goes particularly well.
Retail price: $18
Winemaker: Jeffrey Grosset

Technical data: The fruit is sourced from vineyards in the Polish Hill region and in particular from Jeff's own Gaia vineyard, the highest vineyard in the Clare Valley at 570m. These vineyards are planted on relatively poor, (compared to Watervale) slightly acid soils which requires special vineyard management. This includes some of the most advanced crop canopy management in the region and minimal chemical interference.

Henschke "Julius" Riesling (Eden Valley) preBM

A classic Eden valley Riesling typically with steely acid along with limey and floral characteristics.

Aging potential: 3-8 years
Greatest vintages still drinking well: '79, '82, '87, '90, '92, '93, '94
Recommended food match: Pate, entrees, fish, especially trout, pasta, chicken and antipasto.
Retail price: $16
Winemaker: Stephen Henschke

Howard Park Riesling (Mount Barker) BM

I have been an avid fan of John Wade's wines since his stint as the winemaker for Wynns in the early 80's. In describing this Riesling he modestly wrote "Crisp refreshing style which has firm acidity, and pronounced lime/citrus characters when young, and if left to age, will develop rich toasty flavours." I might add that it has quickly established itself as WA's, and one of Australia's, finest Rieslings. It typically exhibits a wonderful balance of all components as well as the ability to age and develop over the long term.

Aging potential: 7-10 years
Greatest vintages still drinking well: '86, '90, '91, '94
Winemasker's food match: Seafood, aperitifs, entree dishes
Retail price: $18
Winemaker: John Wade

Technical data: Only free-run juice is used to produce this wine.

*Knights Granite Hills Riesling (Macedon) preBM

Intensely flavoured, limey Riesling that can, in the years less affected by botrytis, age wonderfully developing toast and honey characters.

Aging potential: 5-10 years
Greatest vintages still drinking well: '86, '90, '91, '93
Retail price: $14
Winemaker: Lew Knight

Leo Buring "Leonay" Eden Valley Riesling (Eden Valley) BM

A fresh, restrained wine showing lemon citrus fruit and steely, firm acidity. This classy wine is traditionally not as full flavoured as its Clare Valley counterpart and therefore benefits greatly from time in the bottle, when some toasty, honeyed richness will develop.

Aging potential: 10-20 years (in great vintages will live considerably longer).
Greatest vintages still drinking well: '72, '73, '75, '79, '80, '90, '91, '94
Winemaker's food match: Seafood dishes, white meat dishes, Chinese and Japanese dishes or by itself.
Retail price: $17
Winemaker: Robert Ruediger and John Vickery (Up to '93)

Technical data: The King of Australian Riesling; John Vickery, is now at Richmond Grove and the quality of that company's wines can only improve as a result.

Leo Buring "Leonay" Watervale Riesling (Clare Valley) BM

A soft yet full flavoured style showing lime juice fruit flavours and aromas, rose petal like characters and crisp acidity. These wines develop far more rapidly than their Eden Valley counterparts and hence show a lovely dollop of bottle age aromas and flavours (toast, lime and aged Riesling complexity) when released at three years of age. A complex and beautifully balanced Riesling showing great depth of flavour and representing the pinnacle of white wine making in this country.

Aging potential: 10-20 years (And more in great vintages).
Greatest vintages still drinking well: '72, '73, '75, '78, '88, '90, '91, '93, '94
Winemaker's food match: Seafood, white meat, vegetarian and Asian cuisine or by itself.
Retail price: $17
Winemaker: '93 and before: John Vickery, From '94 vintage: Geoff Henriks

*Mitchell Watervale Riesling (Clare Valley) BM

One of this region's best. Steely acid and a crisp, austere palate often reminds me of the Eden Valley. Floral aromas are typical as are lime and other citrus fruits on the palate. Wonderfully fresh drinking when young it will none the less repay cellaring over the long term.

Aging potential: 5-10 years
Greatest vintages still drinking well: '78, '82, '84, '86, '87, '90, '91, '92, '93, '94, '95
Retail price: $14
Winemaker: Andrew Mitchell

Mitchelton Riesling (Goulburn Valley) preBM

The style of this wine has varied little during the last 15 years. The aroma typically shows lemon blossom along with some floral highlights and a hint of spiciness. The palate has an abundance of sweet, rich fruit balanced by zesty acidity. It is undoubtedly one of the best value Rieslings on the market.

Aging potential: The structure of this wine makes it ideal for current consumption but history has shown that up to 15 years bottle maturation can benefit the better vintages.
Greatest vintages still drinking well: '81, '83, '85, '87, '91, '93, '94
Recommended food match: Seafood, Asian dishes, fresh water fish and yabbies.
Retail price: $12
Winemaker: Don Lewis

Technical Data: The final acid in the wine is usually about 8.5 grams/litre and this is balanced by 4-5gm/litre of residual sugar. A neutral yeast is used for fermentation that occurs at around 10 degrees Celsius.

Orlando Steingarten Riesling (Eden Valley) BM

One of the most distinctive and talked about Rieslings in Australia. Talked about firstly, in regards to the enormous cost in establishing the Steingarten vineyard and secondly, as too whether or not it was worth it. Time has shown that it was so. Typically exhibits floral aromas and intense yet delicate lime characters. The finish is usually long and very dry.

Aging potential: 6-8 years
Greatest vintages still drinking well: '86, '87, '88, '90, '92, '94
Winemaker's food match: Excellent with grilled seafood
Retail price: $18
Winemaker: Philip Laffer.

Orlando St Helga Riesling (Eden Valley) preBM

Typically a clean, Riesling with lemon/lime characters and crisp, dry acid. Generally represents outstanding value for money.

Aging potential: 5 years
Greatest vintages still drinking well: '86, '87, '88, '89, '90, '92, '93
Winemaker's food match: Fish, mussels, oysters
Retail price: $10
Winemaker: Philip Laffer

Petaluma Riesling (Clare Valley) BM

A dry, "late picked" style with full Riesling flavours (lime, passion fruit) fairly high alcohol (giving the palate a viscosity) and a crisp citrussy finish.

Aging potential: 5 - 20 years (great vintages only)
Greatest vintages still drinking well: '80, '90, '93, '87, '84, '86, '91, '95
Retail price: $19
Winemaker: Brian Croser

Technical data: Petaluma's "Hanlin Hill" vineyard is the highest vineyard in the Clare Valley. The low yielding, 20 year old Riesling vines are hand picked.

Pikes Riesling (Clare Valley) BM

A crisp, fine and dry Riesling that typically shows the aromas and flavours of lime, orange and lemon blossom, other citrus fruits, and a spicy character. In cooler years the wine is known to get a slight marmalade character.

Aging potential: 5-10 years+
Greatest vintages still drinking well: '85, '86, '91 to '94
Winemaker's food match: Oysters, delicate fish dishes.
Retail price: $12
Winemaker: Neil Pike

*Pipers Brook Riesling (Pipers Brook, Tasmania) BM

An outstanding example of cool climate Riesling. Floral aromas are typical of the bouquet along with a soft limey palate with the delicious nuances of grass and fresh herbs.

Aging potential: 4-8 years
Greatest vintages still drinking well: '85, '86, '89, '90, '91 '92, '93 '94 '95
Retail price: $18
Winemaker: Dr Andrew Pirie

*Tim Knappstein Riesling (Clare Valley) BM

Lime and citrus flavours are typically balanced by crisp, lively acidity. Good balance and delicacy of flavour are hallmarks here. Consistently one the Clare's finest and best value Rieslings.

Aging potential: 4-8 years+
Greatest vintages still drinking well: '81, '85, '86, '88, '90, '93, '94, '95
Retail price: $13
Winemaker: Andrew Hardy

DRY RIESLINGS - A CLASS OF THEIR OWN

Tollana Eden Valley Riesling V

This wine can often show a delicate rose petal aroma when young. The palate typically has ripe lime\citrus flavours and finishes with fresh crisp acidity.

Aging potential: 7-10 years After two years in the bottle the wine will develop a lovely toasty character which continues to build for anything up to, and beyond, ten years
Greatest vintages still drinking well: '76, '79, '84, '87, '90, '94
Winemaker's food match: White meats, fresh water yabbies or any seafood, Lightly spiced Asian dishes
Retail price: $10
Winemaker: Neville Falkenberg

Technical data: Sourced from 20-25 year old vines which adds intensity. The grapes are harvested at dusk, crushed immediately, and the juice is drained away from skins to prevents the extraction of any coarseness.

*Wolf Blass Gold Label Riesling BM

Despite this makers reputation for reds, in recent years this has been my favourite Blass wine. Typically intense, with limey Riesling characters filling out a soft, round palate. Crisp acid is balanced by a hint of sweetness on the lingering finish.

Aging potential: 3-8 years
Greatest vintages still drinking well: '88, '90, '91 '92, '93, '95
Retail price: $16
Winemaker: John Glaetzer

Wynns Coonawarra Riesling V

Typically a flavoursome, yet delicate Riesling with ripe flavours (floral, citrus, and apple), zesty acid, and a touch of residual sugar on the finish. In great years such as '94, this wine is as good as Riesling under $10 gets.

Aging potential: 1-4 years typically (great years can live for ten years plus)
Greatest vintages still drinking well: '82, '87, '92, '94
Winemaker's food match: Asian style foods such as Thai, salads and antipasto
Retail price: $10
Winemaker: Peter Douglas

Technical data: Fermented in stainless steel tanks at relatively cool temperatures. It is stabilised and bottled as soon as possible after vintage.

Other Recommended Producers: Chateau Tahbilk, Heggies, Alkoomi, Castle Rock, Pewsey Vale, Plantagenet, Seppelt, amongst others

PERFUMED & DRY - THE AROMATICS

The Sauvignon Blanc and Classic Dry whites listed here have abundant fruit aromas and flavours yet finish relatively dry ie: there is generally little (if any) fermentable sugar left in the wine. Although some of these wines have undergone partial, new oak treatment, the influence is only subtle and they remain refreshing, zesty wines. For information on Gewurztraminer See Pg 48.

A short note on Sauvignon Blanc. Most wine glossaries will sum up this highly fashionable variety by asserting that it does not age well, and therefore should be consumed while young, fresh, and fruity. However, anyone who has tasted a 15 year old Haut Brion Blanc (Sauvignon/Semillon blend), a Cullen Sauvignon Blanc at 5 years, or the '80 Katnook Sauvignon Blanc (still drinking brilliantly) knows the danger of such generalisations. As with all things vinous, it is a matter of personal taste as to whether you will prefer Sauvignon Blanc with some bottle age, or when young and zesty. The Australian Sauvignon Blancs that are capable of aging will shed their overt perfumed characters for more delicate spicy nuances as well as traces of honey and toast. They can represent remarkably refined drinking and are far better food wines than when young. They are however, relatively few in number and it is therefore important to note the winemaker's recommendations.

LEGEND OF SYMBOLS

"BM" - stands for bench-mark. Wines titles that are followed by this symbol are wines to measure others by.
"preBM" - indicates a wine that has shown itself capable of achieving a BM standard however the 'label' lacks either a long enough history of vintages or perhaps the consistency to be titled as such.
"V" - stands for Value. These wines represent very good examples of their region and/or wine style, and are relatively inexpensive (at least under $20).
"*" - the author has compiled this wine description with little if any feed-back from the producer.

*Alkoomi Classic White (Frankland River) V

Typically a pungent dry white with generous flavour (gooseberries and asparagus) and vibrant acid on the crisp finish.

Aging potential: Drink now
Greatest vintages still drinking well: '93, '94, '95, '96
Retail price: $13
Winemaker: Kim Hart

*Bridgewater Mill Sauvignon Blanc (SA) preBM

This wine has quickly established itself as one of the better South Australian examples of this variety. Typically a well judged blend of grassy and tropical fruit characters with a crisp finish.

Aging potential: Should be consumed within the first couple of years after release
Greatest vintages still drinking well: '93 '94, '95
Retail price: $16
Winemaker: Brian Croser

Cape Clairault Semillon Sauvignon Blanc (Margaret River) V

A richly flavoured style with a soft, rounded mouthfeel and crisp acidity on the finish. The flavours are predominantly those of citrus fruits and passionfruit.

Aging potential:: 3-5 years
Greatest vintages still drinking well: '85, '86, '88, '91, '92, '94(best yet)
Winemaker's food match: Fish and chips, Morton Bay bugs, Thai salad and other spicy dishes, B.B.Qed prawns.
Retail price:$16
Winemaker: Ian Lewis

Technical data: No oak is used.

Capel Vale Semillon/Sauvignon Blanc (Capel WA) V

Medium body, dry, but fruit rich style that typically shows kiwi fruit and gooseberry characters along with a touch of herbaceous/grassy/peapod flavours. These aromas carry on to a generous mid palate and a clean crisp finish.

Aging potential:: Ideally consumed when young and fresh, this wine will however gain "honeyed toast" richness with bottle age.
Greatest vintages still drinking well: '85, '91, '93, '94, '95
Winemaker's food match: best with seafood, fish, salads; an ideal luncheon wine.
Retail price: $14
Winemaker: Rob Bowen

Technical data: No oak is used.

Cape Mentelle Semillon\Sauvignon Blanc (Margaret River) preBM

A medium bodied wine with fresh fruit (herbaceous, passionfruit\ fig and citrus) flavours and aromas. In cooler years the emphasis will be on the former descriptives, in warmer years - the latter.

Aging potential: Best consumed within 12 months of vintage.
Greatest vintages still drinking well: Current vintages.
Winemaker's food match: Seafood dishes, antipasto platters or anywhere, anytime.
Retail price: $18
Winemaker: David Hohnen & John Durham

Technical data: 35% of the wine is fermented in new oak barrels and left on lees for 2-3 months. This results in a very subtle oak influence (a gentle chalkiness in the mouth)

Cullen Sauvignon Blanc
(See FULL FLAVOURED, DRY WHITES with oak influence Pg 163)

Evans & Tate WA Classic V

A skilful blend of Semillon and Sauvignon Blanc sourced from the premium, cooler South Western regions of Western Australia. Bottled early to retain freshness, this style typically exhibits a combination of passionfruit/tropical flavours balanced by delicate, refreshing acidity and a crisp dry finish.

Aging potential: Drink now.
Greatest vintages still drinking well: Current vintages.
Winemaker's food match: Australian seafood or Oriental foods such as Thai.
Retail price: $17
Winemaker: Brian Fletcher

Houghton Show Reserve White Burgundy (Swan Valley, WA) BM
[Soon to have a name change]
Each year at least 1000 cases of the Houghton "White Burgundy" are reserved for exhibition in wine shows. This wine is generally released at six years of age with a swag of Gold medals and trophies added to its name. With its extra bottle age the wine has developed a golden colour and a rich honeyed, toasty bouquet. The palate has developed an extra dimension of richness, softness and further complexity.

Aging potential: Released in its prime although will generally hold for several years.
Greatest vintages still drinking well: '86, '84, '82, '87, '89, '91,'93
Suggested food match: seafood, spicy foods and other Asian cuisines.
Retail price: $25
Winemaker: Paul Lapsley

Houghton White Burgundy (Swan Valley, WA) preBM
[Soon to have a name change]

Softness and fullness of flavour are hallmarks of this wine. Ripe fruit flavours are balanced beautifully by crisp, clean acidity and toasty, slightly resinous oak. This wine is continually underrated by many serious wine drinkers, despite it winning many show awards and despite the ravings of wine writers. This may be due to its unfortunate labelling as "White Burgundy" as many wine buyers associate such French generic labels with lesser quality wines.

Aging potential: Excellent, it usually takes 5 - 6 years to reach its peak yet the greatest vintages will live much longer. Despite this, it is delicious when young and fresh and you should not be afraid to drink it as such.
Greatest vintages still drinking well: '86, '84, '82, '87, '89, '91,'93
Winemaker's food match: seafood, spicy foods and other Asian cuisines.
Retail price: $12
Winemaker: Paul Lapsley

Technical data: The complexity of the wine is achieved by the blending of several grape varieties, in descending order of importance; Chenin Blanc, Muscadelle, Chardonnay, and sometimes Verdelho and Semillon. Further interest is achieved by oak fermentation. A proportion of the blend is always fermented and aged in small oak barriques (mostly French and some American)

*Katnook Sauvignon Blanc (Coonawarra) BM

Australia's finest expression of Sauvignon Blanc. Young examples of this wine are typically bursting with passionfruit, gooseberry and asparagus characters balanced by vibrant acidity. With age, the tropical fruit characters slowly subside, disappearing at around six or seven years, making way for honey and toast development that in turn subsides for smoky, spicy nuances and more austerity on the palate. In short the wine sheds its overt fruitiness and becomes crisper, more complex and, as winemaker Wayne Stehbens is keen to point out, far better suited to a wide range of foods. It is an evolution from a 'summer and shellfish' wine, to a table wine of the highest order.

Aging potential: Excellent, the 1980 Katnook Sauvignon Blanc has only recently reached its peak. I tried it in early 1996 and it was strikingly reminiscent of the great '80 Haut Brion White Bordeaux.
Greatest vintages still drinking well: '80, '82, '86, '87, '88, '90, '91, '92, '94 '95. However, all vintages make for excellent drinking and show no sign of tiring.
Retail price: $24
Winemaker: Wayne Stehbens

Lenswood Sauvignon Blanc
(See Crisp & Dry section Pg 139)

Mount Avoca Sauvignon Blanc (Pyrenees) preBM

Fresh Sauvignon Blanc aromas typically abound and although quite ripe in character (packed with sweet tropical/melon fruit flavours and with relative high alcohol) there is a subtle grassy streak running through the wine. Full flavoured with a crisp finish and a soft lingering aftertaste.

Aging potential: generally drunk young, but will age for 6-8years.
Greatest vintages: '87, '93, '94
Winemaker's food match: Seafood, Thai/Asian food
Retail price: $17
Winemaker: Rodney Morrish

Technical data: Immediate drainage of juice followed by cold enzyme settling prior to fermentation with EC 1118 "Prise de Mousse" yeast. The wine undergoes cool fermentation in temperature controlled stainless steel tanks at between twelve and fifteen degrees Celsius.

Mount Mary "Triolet"
(See Crisp & Dry section Pg 141)

*Pierro Semillon/Sauvignon Blanc L.T.C (Margaret River) preBM

A lovely soft, rounded style with creamy tropical and gooseberry flavours and a lingering dry finish.

Aging potential: 2-4 years
Greatest vintages still drinking well: '91,'92, '93, '94, '96
Retail price: $17
Winemaker: Michael Peterkin

Pikes Sauvignon Blanc (Clare Valley) preBM

A fresh non-wooded style exhibiting warm climate Sauvignon Blanc characters (tropical fruit\stone fruit with perhaps some citrus and grassiness) with zesty, spicy acidity. An intensely flavoured wine that manages also to be fresh and crisp.

Aging potential: 2-4 years.
Greatest vintages still drinking well: '93, '94
Winemaker's food match: From Asian to Oysters, Chilli, Crabs and lobster.
Retail price: $14
Winemaker: Neil Pike

*Rochecombe Sauvignon Blanc preBM

An outstanding Sauvignon that is noted for its intense green pea & gooseberry characteristics, spicy acidity and its bone dry finish. Very difficult to find on the mainland due to its tiny production. May merit BM status in future editions.

Aging potential: Should be consumed within the first couple of years after release
Greatest vintages still drinking well: '91 '93
Retail price: $25
Winemaker: Bernard Rochaix

*Schinus Sauvignon Blanc preBM

Typically a stylish wine that is invariable crisp and zesty, exhibiting a fine balance of all components.

Aging potential: Should be consumed within the first couple of years after release
Greatest vintages still drinking well: '90, '91,'92, '95
Retail price: $16
Winemaker: Gary Crittenden

*Shaw & Smith Sauvignon Blanc (Adelaide Hills) BM

Typically a richly flavoured Sauvignon with round, mouthfilling gooseberry flavours balanced by a streak of grassiness and crisp acid on the finish.

Aging potential:: Although generally preferred young, this wine can develop with age.
Greatest vintages still drinking well: '93, '94, '95
Retail price: $18
Winemaker: Martin Shaw

*Stafford Ridge Sauvignon Blanc (Adelaide Hills-Lenswood) preBM

Pungent varietal aromas and a soft, round palate are typical of this classy wine.

Aging potential:: 1-4 years
Greatest vintages still drinking well: '91, '92, '93, '94
Retail price: $19
Winemaker: Geoff Weaver

Vasse Felix Classic Dry White (Margaret River) preBM

The richness of this wine can vary between vintages ('93 for example exhibits more pungent grassiness than '94) but generally a good balance is struck between the herbaceous characters of capsicum and grass, and those in the tropical fruit spectrum (melon, lychee, honey). Typically finishes with crisp, sherbet-like acid.

Aging potential: 1 year
Greatest vintages still drinking well: '92, '94
Winemaker's food match: seafood, light meats-chicken, rabbit, Asian food.
Retail price: $18
Winemaker: Clive Otto

Technical data: A blend of Semillon, Sauvignon Blanc, and Chardonnay with minimal oak treatment.

*Wirra Wirra Sauvignon Blanc (McLaren Vale) preBM

Typically a pristine example of McLaren Vale Sauvignon with flavours in the tropical spectrum along with a trace of herbaceousness. The palate is characteristically full flavoured and soft with cleansing acid.

Aging potential: Should be consumed within the first couple of years after release
Greatest vintages still drinking well: '89, '91, '92, '94
Retail price: $15
Winemaker: Ben Riggs

Yarra Ridge Sauvignon Blanc (Yarra Valley) preBM

Typically a lush, fresh dry white with herbal and tropical fruit flavours. A hint of sweetness on the finish is balanced by good acidity.

Aging potential: 1-2years
Greatest vintages still drinking well: '91, '92, '94
Winemaker's food match: Seafood. fish, vegetable dishes, Asian cuisines
Retail price: $16
Winemaker: Louis Bialkower & Rob Dolan

Other Recommended Producers: Cullen (Classic Dry), Sauvignon Blancs:
Gembrook estate, Salitage, Hill Smith Estate,
Leeuwin Estate, amongst others

FULL FLAVOURED DRY WHITES

With Oak Influence

Generally speaking, this category represents our most powerful and richly flavoured dry whites. There is substantial variation in both the weight and style of wines listed here, ranging from crisp, and restrained in flavour, to super rich, powerhouses of oak and viscous fruit. For this reason, close readings of the wine descriptions are required. The flavour characteristics endowed by oak treatment has been discussed in detail on page 22. Needless to say, the best oak treated white wines are those where the oak plays an enhancing, rather than a dominant, role. Hence with many of the wines listed here, there is not a distinctive oaky character but rather little hints in the background. A trace of vanilla, a whiff of toast. etc. There is also the dimension of weight and complexity that oak treatment adds to a wine. Whilst many Australian wine styles still lack the recognition they deserve, many of our wooded whites are only now beginning to justify their reputation.

LEGEND OF SYMBOLS

"BM" - stands for bench-mark. Wines titles that are followed by this symbol are wines to measure others by.
"preBM" - indicates a wine that has shown itself capable of producing wines of a BM standard however the 'label' lacks either a long enough history of vintages or perhaps the consistency to be titled as such.
"V" - stands for Value. These wines represent very good examples of their region and/or wine style, and are relatively inexpensive (at least under $20).
"*" - the author has compiled this wine description with little if any feed-back from the producer.

*Bannockburn Chardonnay (Geelong) BM

Typically a richly flavoured, powerful wine that runs the gamut of ripe Chardonnay flavours and aromas (melon\peach,etc.) along with exhibiting the toasty oak and barrel fermentation characteristics (butterscotch, nuts) that help give the wine its depth of flavour.

Aging potential: This wine will generally benefit from 3-6 years of cellaring and will often live and develop longer.
Greatest vintages still drinking well: '84, '85, '87, '88, '90, '91, '92, '93, '94
Retail price: $33
Winemaker: Garry Farr

*Basedows White Burgundy [Semillon] (Barossa) V

A full flavoured white that is noted for its abundance of flavour (honey, grassy fruit and lots of toasty oak) as well as for being outstanding value for money. Great with roast chicken.

Aging potential: 2-5 years
Greatest vintages still drinking well: '90, '91, '92, '94, '95
Retail price: $12
Winemaker: Doug Lehmann

Capel Vale Chardonnay (Capel, Mount Barker) BM

Typically a complex, luscious and full bodied wine with layers of flavour. The dominant fruit characteristics are melon, peach, passionfruit and guava with cashew nut, oak characters. There is also an intriguing herbaceousness that marries perfectly with the wines richer elements. It is one of the more interesting Chardonnays on the market evolving in the glass so that with each sip the taster is surprised by new characteristics, as though they were now tasting a different wine.

Aging potential: 4-12 yrs
Greatest vintages still drinking well: '86, '88, '92, '93, '94
Winemaker's food match: Most light meat dishes, entrees, seafood
Retail price: $20
Winemaker: Rob Bowen & Krister Jonsson

Technical data: The Chardonnay grapes that go into making this wine are deliberately picked at differing levels of ripeness to gain complexity of flavours. 1/3rd of the wine undergoes barrel fermentation and is matured on its lees for 9 months. 1/3rd of the wine undergoes malo-lactic fermentation. 1, 2, and 3 year old oak barrels from a variety of French forests are used.

Capel Vale Special Reserve "Frederick" Chardonnay (Capel, WA) preBM

A small quantity of Capel Vale's very best Chardonnay was put aside in the '92 and '94 vintages and given high class French oak, and lees handling, to produce Reserve wines of exceptional quality and cellaring potential. These are full bodied wines that are most accurately described as a richer, more concentrated versions of the 'standard' Capel Vale Chardonnay exhibiting more overt barrel fermentation characters and an almost honeyed richness. As only two vintages have been released at the time of writing it is too early to grant the wine a BM rating despite its quality.

Aging potential: 5-12 years
Greatest vintages still drinking well: '92, '94 (only vintages so far)
Winemaker's food match: This wine may be enjoyed on its own but will enhance the flavours of both white meat and light red meat dishes.
Retail price: $40
Winemaker: Rob Bowen & Krister Jonsson

Technical data: Produced entirely from Chardonnay grapes grown on Capel Vale's Capel, Wellington and Stirling Vineyards. The Chardonnay fruit that goes into this wine is picked at varying stages of ripening to maximise flavour complexity. 100% of the wine is barrel fermented and kept on gross lees for 9 months in barriques, 1-4 years old, from a variety of French coopers and French forests mainly Vosges and Allier.

Cape Mentelle Chardonnay (Margaret River) BM

From a winery best known for its outstanding red wines comes this delicious wine that David Hohnen modestly describes as "an intriguing dry white". Citrus and peach aromas typically combine with pronounced toast and butterscotch characters on a concentrated, yet soft and supple palate.

Aging potential: 3-5 years
Greatest vintages still drinking well: '90, '93, '94
Winemaker's food match: Atlantic Salmon with fava bean puree and grilled leeks.
Retail price: $24
Winemaker: David Hohnen & John Durham

FULL FLAVOURED DRY WHITES

Cassegrain Fromenteau Chardonnay (Hastings Valley) BM

A complex, full flavoured dry white which often shows intense aromas of peach and melon fruit, and in, riper years, pineapple, citrus and spice. The palate is generally powerful yet restrained with very attractive honey, peach and toasted oak flavours.

Aging potential: 4-15 years
Greatest vintages still drinking well: '86, '89, '91 ('93 is showing a great deal of promise).
Winemaker's food match: Poached salmon and richly flavoured seafood dishes in general (lobster - shellfish). Veal in a cream based sauce.
Retail price: $28
Winemaker: John Cassegrain and Drew Noon

Technical data: A single vineyard wine, 100% of the grapes are sourced from Cassegrain's 7 acre "Fromenteau" vineyard. The yield is a low, 2.5 tonnes per acre. The wine is fermented and matured on lees for ten months in French oak Barriques. In some years a portion of the wine may undergo a malo-lactic fermentation. After being bottled, the wine is cellared for several years prior to its release.

Coldstream Hills "Reserve" Chardonnay (Yarra Valley) BM

One of the Yarra Valley's finest examples of Chardonnay this wine is typically richly flavoured, with a multitude of Chardonnay characteristics and toasty/cedary oak. It characteristically exhibits a 'tightness', due to its balance and finely crafted acid structure, that ensures longevity.

Aging potential: 4-8 years
Greatest vintages still drinking well: '88, '90, '91, '92, '93, '94
Retail price: $34
Winemaker: James Halliday and Phillip Dowell

Cullen Chardonnay (Margaret River) BM

An enormous, mouth filling Chardonnay with great depth and class that typically exhibits ripe fruit flavours (grapefruit, melon) combined with spicy, toasty oak.

Aging potential: 5-10 years
Greatest vintages still drinking well: '82, '85, '88, '92, '93, '94
Winemaker's food match: Creamy pasta dishes, chicken, shellfish
Retail price: $28
Winemaker: Vanya Cullen

Cullen Sauvignon Blanc (Margaret River) BM

Ultra-ripe Sauvignon Blanc that typically exhibits tropical fruit characteristics along with a streak of grassiness and subtle nutty oak characters. The palate structure is creamy and long with perfect oak handling and cleansing acid on the finish.

Aging potential: 3-7 years
Greatest vintages still drinking well: '88 '91, '93
Winemaker's food match: Asparagus, shell fish, Thai food
Retail price: $22
Winemaker: Vanya Cullen

Cullen Semillon/Sauvignon Blanc "Reserve" BM

Fruit flavours typical of the region (gooseberry, lemon, grassy, herbaceous) are enhanced by round, barrel ferment characters and spicy oak. A rich, ripe style that shows excellent integration of fruit and oak.

Aging potential: 5 yrs
Greatest vintages still drinking well: '92, '93
Winemaker's food match: seafood, chicken, asparagus
Retail: $25
Winemaker: Vanya Cullen

Technical data: Viticultural techniques are essentially organic. The fruit is picked ripe to balance the savoury fruit flavours of these two grape varieties. The wine undergoes barrel fermented and lees aging prior to bottling.

Evans & Tate Chardonnay (Margaret River) BM

Typically a beautifully structured wine that exhibits mouthfilling Chardonnay fruit flavours (peach, tropical fruits, nuts) and spicy French oak characters in support. Intensely flavoured yet crisp and elegant Margaret River Chardonnay.

Aging potential: 5 yrs
Greatest vintages: '91, '92, '93, '94, '95
Retail price: $22
Winemaker: Brian Fletcher

Technical data: Evans & Tate Margaret River Chardonnay is produced from the best fruit grown on the Redbrook Estate vineyards. Only high quality French oak is used.

Evans & Tate Semillon BM

The typically zesty straw and tropical/citrus fruit flavours of this wine are enhanced by cradle of toasty, spicy French oak.

Aging potential: Delicious when fresh and young this wine will develop rich honey, nuts, and buttery characters with 3-5 years of bottle aging
Greatest vintages still drinking well: '89, '90, '91, '92, '93, '94, '95
Winemaker's food match: Perfect with seafood, especially mudcrabs.
Retail price: $20
Winemaker: Brian Fletcher

Technical data: 100% Margaret River, this wine undergoes barrel fermentation in the finest French oak

Giaconda Chardonnay (Beechworth) BM

One of Australiaís greatest, yet least known, Chardonnays, this wine typically exhibits the complex aromas of quince like Chardonnay fruit, along with nuts and mealy yeast characters while the palate is normally very concentrated, powerful and long with a lingering touch of toasty oak. It is a wine that is all about power with elegance.

Aging potential: One of the few Australian Chardonnays built to last so try to give it at least 5 years cellaring and more in the better years when it will easily live and develop beyond 10 years.
Greatest vintages still drinking: '90, '91, '92, '93
Winemaker's food match: Seafood, etc.
Retail price: $28
Winemaker: Rick Kinzbrunner

Technical data: This Chardonnay is sourced from a low cropping, vineyard that has an altitude of 400 metres plus a southerly aspect. The soil is gravel with about 50% clay in the subsoil. Traditional (Burgundian) winemaking techniques are used, including natural yeast, full malo-lactic fermentation, long ageing on lees in the very best French oak (40% new). The wine spends around 18 months in barrel prior to bottling.

*Goonawarra Semillon (Sunbury, Macedon) preBM

This crisp, flavoursome wine is one of the most distinctive Semillons produced in this country. It shows plenty of honeyed fruit with toasty, cedary oak flavours, yet despite this richness it remains crisp and tight with a restrained mouthfeel.

Aging potential: 3-6 years
Greatest vintages still drinking well: '89, '91, '93, '94
Retail price: $18
Winemaker: John Barnier

*Grant Burge Chardonnay (Barossa) preBM

A full bodied, richly flavoured wine typically packed with juicy Chardonnay and toasty oak. Pristine varietal characteristics and stylish oak, that in no way dominates the fruit, separates this wine from others in its price range.

Aging potential: 3-6 years
Greatest vintages still drinking: '93, '94, '95
Retail price: $14
Winemaker: Grant Burge

Grosset Piccadilly Chardonnay (Piccadilly, Adelaide Hills) preBM

Most of Grosset's Chardonnays, pre '94 vintage, were made from predominantly Clare Valley fruit. 20% of Adelaide Hills fruit was used in '90, gradually increasing to 100% in '94. Typically an intense yet elegant Chardonnay with classy, subtle oak handling lending spicy oak nuances. Quickly heading for BM status.

Aging potential: 5-8 years.
Greatest vintages still drinking well: '94, '95
Retail price: $25
Winemaker: Jeffrey Grosset

*Hardys Eileen Hardy Chardonnay (Padthaway\Yarra Valley) BM

Typically an intense, richly flavoured Chardonnay that has the fruit weight to match its substantial oak characteristics. A big wine that is none the less very classy and all the better for its Yarra Valley component.

Aging potential: A fine aging style that will typically benefit from 5 -10 years in bottle.
Greatest vintages still drinking: '85, '86, '89, '90, '91, '92, '93
Retail price: $23
Winemaker: Tom Newton

Henschke Semillon (Eden Valley/Keyneton) BM

Typically, a rich, mouthfilling wine that exhibits a creamy texture and the seductive characteristics of honeyed toast, vanilla, freshly mown hay and gooseberry.

Aging potential: 4-8 years
Greatest vintages: '86, '88, '89, '91, '92, '93
Winemaker's food match: Seafood, especially trout, chicken, duck or pork
Retail price: $18
Winemaker: Stephen Henschke

FULL FLAVOURED DRY WHITES

Lake's Folly Chardonnay (Lower Hunter Valley) BM

The Hunter, with its warm to hot climate, continues to disprove the theory that high quality Chardonnay can only come from cool climate regions. This wine is the perfect antithesis to such arguments. It typically shows ripe fruit characteristics (Fig, melon, peach, guava) balanced by a good acid structure and sweet, well integrated oak.

Aging potential: 5-12 years. On average this wine peaks at around 7 years of age.
Greatest vintages still drinking well: '81, '83, '86, '89, '93, '94 (the best yet!)
Winemaker's food match: Stephen Lake suggests that there are no such rules to go with his wine, simply drink it before you start on the red wine and at "not too cold" a temperature (approx. 15celcius)
Retail price: $30
Winemaker: Stephen Lake

Leeuwin Estate Chardonnay (Margaret River) BM

The benchmark for new world Chardonnays, this wine is typically well balanced yet complex, with a delicacy of texture that belies its weight. Almost viscous in the mouth, it characteristically coats the tongue with subtle tropical fruit flavours (pineapple usually predominant) with pear and sweet hazelnut overtones. This richness is balanced by a firm acidity that cleans the palate and ensures longevity. A sublime balancing act between power and finesse.

Aging potential: Well known for its ability to age, the earliest vintages of this wine are still drinking well! Needs at least 8-10 years to come into its own and will live and often develop for significantly longer periods.
Greatest vintages still drinking well: '81, '82, '87, '92, '93 (Don't write off the lessor years!)
Winemaker's food match: As a young wine (5-8 years), the stronger seafood dishes eg. Lobster, Thermidor. As a mature wine (8 years+), fine with juicy poultry.
Retail price: $49
Winemaker: Robert G. Cartwright.

Technical data: The Chardonnay grapes that go into making this wine are 100% estate grown and the Leeuwin vineyards are planted solely with the Gin Gin variety of Chardonnay. No chemical fertilisers are used in the vineyards, only mulch and green manure crops. The wine is barrel fermented and matured in 100% new French oak (a mixture of Troncais, Allier, Vosges-medium toast) on lees for around 18 months.

Leeuwin Prelude Chardonnay (Margaret River) preBM

A crisper, less opulent wine than the 'Art Series' Chardonnay, this wine is none the less characteristically full of soft, creamy Chardonnay flavours with subtle oak characters and zesty acidity.

Aging potential: 3-8 years.
Retail price: $21
Winemaker: Robert G. Cartwright.

Technical data: This wine typically spends around 9 months in barrel (Allier/Troncais - 20% new) on lees, with lees stirring. Around 25% undergoes malo-lactic fermentation.

Lefroy Brook Chardonnay (Lower Great Southern) BM

This wine is typically finely structured, lean and complex with a floral bouquet and lime/citrus, subtle apple and flinty, mineral flavours. Fine oak lends spicy, vanillin nuances and the wine finishes crisp and long. This beautifully balanced and elegant wine is perhaps the closest Australia comes to French Chablis. It is also as far away from the stereotypical peaches and cream style of Chardonnay as you could imagine.

Aging potential: The wine is dense and taught in its first two years. Thereafter it ages gracefully gathering added complexity and intensity. Perfect between 7-10 years of age.
Greatest vintages still drinking well: '89, '90, '92, '93
Winemaker's food match: Antipasto, roast quail etc
Retail price: $27
Winemaker: Peter Fimmel

Technical data: The vineyard is very close planted on fertile loam soil that contributes the mineral and apple characters to the wine. Barrel fermentation is followed by 10 months maturation on lees.

Lillydale Yarra Chardonnays (Yarra Valley) V

A gentle, flavoursome wine that typically displays cool climate Chardonnay fruit (Peach and Melon) with a touch of oak and buttery malo-lactic character that gives the wine balance and style.

Aging potential: These wines drink very well when young and fresh while retaining the ability to develop well in the bottle for a number of years. 3 - 6 years.
Greatest vintages still drinking well: '82, '84, '86, '90, '92, '93, '94
Winemaker's food match: Drinks well with seafood and in particular smoked trout.
Retail Price: $15
Winemaker: Jim Brayne

Lindemans Hunter River Chardonnay (Lower Hunter Valley) V

A good value, medium to full bodied Chardonnay that typically exhibits spicy, peach and melon fruit characters integrated with vanillin oak.

Aging potential: 5 years
Greatest vintages still drinking well: '92, '87
Winemaker's food match: Chicken, veal, seafood
Retail price: $14
Winemaker: Patrick Auld

Technical data: This wine undergoes partial barrel fermentation followed by 4-6 months oak maturation.

Main Ridge Chardonnay (Mornington Peninsula) BM

A full bodied wine that typically exhibits intense and multifarious Chardonnay aromas and flavours (in the citrus, melon spectrum) and vanillin oak. Cleansing acidity and a soft velvety finish are also the norm here. Very classy wine.

Aging potential: Needs at least five years to peak and will live for at least ten years- and probably even longer.
Greatest vintages still drinking well: '86, '88, '90, '91, '92, '93
Winemaker's food match: Seafood
Retail price: $30
Winemaker: Nat White

Technical data: Intensity of fruit flavours and fine acidity result from a long, slow ripening period. Low cropping vineyards give the wine extra richness. The vineyards are of deep red soil and are not irrigated. The Scott Henry trellis system is used. Characteristically high in alcohol, this gives the wine a certain fullness and sweetness without any over ripe flavours. The wine is barrel fermented without Sulphur Dioxide in New French barriques (Vosges).

Moorooduc Estate Chardonnay (Mornington Peninsula) BM

Typically a rich and powerful wine showing ripe fruit flavours complexed by secondary characteristics (those derived from barrel fermentation and partial malo-lactic fermentation). A consistent trait of this wine is a rich mid-palate and lingering flavour. Wonderful drinking.

Aging potential: Probably at its best between 3 - 5 years of age.
Greatest vintages still drinking well: '90, '92, '93, '94
Winemaker's food match: Rich seafood dishes such as Salmon and Crayfish, also goes well with light meat.
Retail price: $23
Winemaker: Richard McIntyre

Technical data: The wine is barrel fermented and a proportion goes through malo-lactic fermentation. Fully imported French barriques are used, approximately half of which are new each year. The wine is left on its primary ferment lees until just before bottling and these are stirred regularly.

*Moss Wood Margaret River Semillon (Wood Matured) BM

One of the Margaret Rivers best examples of Semillon this wine typically exhibits a long flavoursome palate packed with gooseberry/tropical fruit married with spicy, vanillin oak and vibrant acidity. Very stylish.

Aging potential: 4-10 years
Greatest vintages still drinking well: '85, '87, '88, '90, '91, '92
Retail price: $20
Winemaker: Keith Mugford

Mountadam Chardonnay (Adelaide Hills) preBM

This wine is noted for its complexity. It typically exhibits ripe, cool climate fruit and barrel fermented characteristics of tropical fruit, grilled nuts, a hint of honey and first class, spicy oak. Mountadam Chardonnay also has a 'tightness' of structure that give the wine a deceptive elegance in the mouth as well as ensuring longevity.

Aging potential: The wine will benefit from 5 years in the bottle and will continue developing for at least 10 years.
Greatest vintages still drinking well: '84, '87, '89, '91, '93
Winemaker's food match: Fish or white meats.
Retail price: $28
Winemaker: Adam Wynn.

Technical data: Made exclusively from grapes grown in Mountadam's low yielding vineyards.

Nicholson River Winery Chardonnay (Gippsland) BM

This is about as powerful as Chardonnay gets. It is typically intensely flavoured and complex with flavours that range from (predominantly) honey, apricot and spice through to melon and toast. An ultra ripe Chardonnay of monolithic proportions with huge weight of flavour in the mouth that leaves the breath scented for minutes after swallowing.

Aging potential: best drunk within 5 years
Greatest vintages: '88, '91, '93, '94
Winemaker's food match: Rich seafood such as smoked salmon
Retail price: Generally not available through retail stores although when it is it sells for around $40.
Cellar door: $25
Winemaker: Ken Eckersley

Technical data: The wines depth of flavour is attributed to Nicholson River having the longest ripening period for Chardonnay in the world (at least 160days from flowering to picking compared to Burgundy; 90 - 100 days). Autumn mists contribute to a slight botrytis character.

Orlando St Hilary Chardonnay (Padthaway) V

Now that its made from 100% Padthaway fruit this wine exhibits a refinement beyond its price and typically shows delicate melon and grapefruit Chardonnay characteristics along with soft nutty oak.

Aging potential: This is not an aging style. Try to drink it up before its 3rd birthday.
Greatest vintages still drinking well: '92, '93, '94
Winemaker's food match: Rich flavoursome seafood and poultry dishes
Retail price: $13
Winemaker: Philip Laffer

Technical data: Matured in a mixture of new and one year old French and American oak.

Petaluma Chardonnay (Piccadilly, Adelaide Hills) BM

A wine that needs little introduction to Australian wine lovers. Perhaps that is why Brian Croser prefers to talk about the great care and attention to detail that goes into making the wine rather than what it tastes like. A very fine, full bodied Chardonnay that never wants for flavour or elegance.

Aging potential: 5-10 years
Greatest vintages still drinking well: ' 86, '87, '88, '89, '90, '91, '92, '94
Retail price: $33
Winemaker: Brian Croser

Technical data: Ripe Chardonnay grapes are hand picked from mature vines and are chilled before pressing as whole bunches. Only the 'heart run' juice of the berries, with high natural acid, sugar and flavour, is used to produce this wine. Fermented in dense oak barriques from the Vosges forest (France), this wine undergoes malo-lactic fermentation, and is stored in barrique, on yeast lees, for one year prior to bottling.

Peter Lehmann Semillon (Barossa) V

Typically a medium bodied dry white that combines fresh lemon/citrus/passionfruit characters with buttery/toasty oak undertones. Consistently good value.

Aging potential: These wines are delightful as youngsters, but as with all good Semillons, up to 5 years bottle maturation will add further depth and complexity.
Greatest vintages still dinking well: '90 - '95
Winemaker's food match: Seafood, poultry and white meat dishes.
Retail price: $12
Winemaker: Peter Lehmann, Andrew Wigan, Peter Scholz and Leonie Lange

Technical data: The grapes that go into making this wine are sourced from a large number of Barossa vineyards which have mature vines, ranging in age from at least 10 to over 60 years of age.

*Pierro Chardonnay (Margaret River) BM

Another of Australia's lessor known, great wines. Pierro Chardonnay has been very consistent since the '86 vintage. It is typically a wine of great sophistication with a tightly knit acid structure interwoven with ripe Chardonnay flavours and nutty oak. One of the Margaret River's finest Chardonnays.

Aging potential: 4-10 years
Greatest vintages still drinking well: '86, '87, '88, '89, '90, '91, '92, '93, '94
Retail price: $34
Winemaker: Mike Peterkin

FULL FLAVOURED DRY WHITES

*Pipers Brook Chardonnay (Pipers Brook) BM

A crisp and elegant Chardonnay whose firm acid structure ensures its superb, aging potential. White peach and citrus fruits are common characteristics with the oak typically lending subtle nuances of spice.

Aging potential: 5-10 years
Greatest vintages still drinking well: '86, '88, '89, '90, '91, '92, '93, '94 (a richer year)
Retail price: $26
Winemaker: Andrew Pirie

Plantagenet Mount Barker Chardonnay (Lower Great Southern) preBM

A medium bodied yet fully flavoured and complex wine that typically shows essence-like ripe Chardonnay aromas (tinned peach, melon), a restrained palate (lemon citrus, peach flavours) and well integrated oak that lends the wine a spicy (nutmeg) character.

Aging potential: 5-8 years
Greatest vintages still drinking well: '89, '90, '93, '94
Winemaker's food match: full flavoured fish dishes, pork.
Retail price: $22
Winemaker: Gavin Berry

Technical data: Fermented in a mixture of new, one and two year old French oak casks and then left on lees for ten months. The wine goes through a secondary or malo-lactic fermentation.

Preece Chardonnay (Goulburn Valley/King Valley) V

A cleverly made wine that typically maximises the fresh peach\ nectarine flavours of Chardonnay with just the right amount of oak treatment contributing butter and nutty nuances. A refreshing style of Chardonnay with good acid and a sweet richness granted by the alcohol (typically around 13%).

Aging potential: Up to 8 years
Greatest vintages still drinking well: '90, '92, '94
Winemaker's food match: Chicken, fish, veal (can handle a fair dose of flavour)
Retail price: $14
Winemaker: Don Lewis

Technical data: Made from grapes mostly grown in Mitchelton's Goulburn Valley vineyard. Moderate crop levels, good irrigation management, and well exposed fruit all play an important role in the vineyard. 20% of the wine is fermented in new oak to add complexity and richness without overpowering the fruit freshness.

Rosemount Diamond Label Chardonnay (Upper Hunter Valley) V

Characteristically exhibits tropical fruit and citrus aromas along with a touch of honey. The palate is very rich with considerable weight of sweet fruit and toasty\vanillin characters imparted from American and French oak maturation. A fruit driven style that oozes flavour.

Aging potential: Ready for consumption on release the wine will hold for up to 5 years depending on vintage.
Greatest vintages still drinking well: '93, '94
Winemaker's food match: Roast chicken, smoked salmon, pasta in light sauces, prawns, scallops
Retail price: $13
Winemaker: Philip Shaw

Rosemount Roxburgh Chardonnay (Upper Hunter) BM

If there was a "White Wine for Heroes" class then this wine would most certainly be in it. Extraordinary richness and depth of flavour are the hallmarks of Roxburgh. Sweet, ripe fruit flavours (in the tropical fruit spectrum), with dried citrus peel, and an oatmeal (yeast) complexity. Oak plays an important role in the structure and flavour of this wine adding smoky vanillin flavours and aromas. Good acid holds everything together, and the wine typically has great length.

Aging potential: Needs 3-5 years to show its true potential and will gracefully develop for another 8-10 years. The older Roxburghs are still holding well.
Greatest vintages still drinking well: '87, '86, '89, '90, '93, '94, '83, '85, '91, '88, '84 (Shaw's order)
Winemaker's food match: Roxburgh suits many fish dishes, charred sword fish and barramundi in particular
Retail price: $40
Winemaker: Philip Shaw

Technical data: The Roxburgh vineyard has a mixture of finely granulated limestone and Terra Rosa (red coloured decomposed limestone) soil. The vines here are hand pruned and hand harvested. The wine undergoes primary fermentation, malo-lactic fermentation, and aging in oak (60% new French, a percentage of American oak and selected older barrels). The level of new oak usage has declined since 1989. The Burgundian method of retaining lees (sediment that settles after fermentation made up of dead yeast cells and grape fragments) in the barrel and stirring them regularly is employed. After 1986 Philip Shaw has made Roxburgh without adding acid (see acidification in Glossary). Since 1988 indigenous yeasts (those native to the vineyard and cellar) have been used to commence fermentation (as opposed to cultured yeasts).

Rosemount Show Reserve Chardonnay (Upper Hunter Valley) preBM

A ripe style of Chardonnay that typically shows honey, tropical fruits and citrus characters intertwined with substantial new oak nuances of toast, vanilla and caramel. The wine normally exhibits a rich creamy mouthfeel, great depth of flavour, and a long, charred-oak finish.

Aging potential: Needs cellaring for 3 years to allow the wine to reach maturity after which it should be drunk over the following 8 years. Top vintages will develop for even longer periods.
Greatest vintages still drinking well: '80, '87, '93, '89, '94
Winemaker's food match: Lobster Bisque, lobster, Marron, yabbies, Quail, turkey and chicken.
Retail price: $21
Winemaker: Philip Shaw

Technical data: The wine is blended from grapes grown in Rosemount's "Roxburgh" (adds richness) and "Giants Creek" (more elegant) Upper Hunter Valley vineyards. The wine undergoes extended lees aging and stirring (battonage). The percentage of new oak varies from 35% - 60% depending on vintage.

Rosemount Show Reserve Semillon (Upper Hunter) preBM

Ripe, rich Semillon fruit flavours (lemon/citrus, wax, and often a touch of grassiness) typically combine with the toastiness of French oak in this mouthfilling white wine. The palate, whilst being substantial in weight, has good firm acidity to balance the richness of flavour.

Aging potential: hold for 3 years to reach maturity before drinking over the next 8 years.
Greatest vintages still drinking well: '80, '87, '93, '89, '94
Winemaker's food match: Seafood in white sauces, fish & chips, Caesar salad, risotto and Veal
Retail price: $20
Winemaker: Philip Shaw

Technical data: A blend of Semillon fruit drawn from Rosemount's Upper Hunter vineyards of "Roxburgh" (adds flesh & power) and "Giants Creek" (More elegant citrus flavours). These vineyards are heavily pruned to produce small crops of intensely flavoured fruit.

Sandstone Semillon (Margaret River) preBM

A flavoursome wine showing ripe fruit flavours and aromas (lemon, peach and tropical fruit) a touch of grassiness and generous, yet full integrated toasty oak.

Aging potential: 3-10 years.
Greatest vintages still drinking well: '88, '91, '93, '94
Winemaker's food match: Shellfish
Retail price:$19
Winemaker: Jan & mike Davies

Technical data: After completing fermentation, 60% of the wine spends six months in new oak (a mixture of French and American) prior to bottling.

Sorrenberg Chardonnay (Beechworth) preBM

Typically a full flavoured yet elegant Chardonnay with a lovely creaminess in the mouth. The oak is well integrated granting the wine a subtle nutty character that never dominates the peach and melon Chardonnay fruit flavours.

Aging potential: 5-8 years
Greatest vintages still drinking well: '90, '91, '94
Winemaker's food match: strong flavoured veal and white meat dishes
Retail price: $23
Winemaker: Barry Morey

Technical data: All Sorrenberg wines are made from grapes grown in the winery's vineyard in Beechworth. The vines grow on granitic soil at around 550 metres above sea level. This 100% Chardonnay is barrel fermented in 30% new and 70% 1-2 year old Burgundian oak. The wine undergoes 100% malo-lactic fermentation. Lees stirring goes on for ten months to give the wine complexity and a more integrated balance of fruit and oak.

*Stonier's Reserve Chardonnay (Mornington Peninsula) BM

Formerly released under the "Merricks" label, this wine typically exhibits ripe, essence like Chardonnay fruit with high class vanillin oak and mealy, yeast complexity.

Aging potential: 5-8 years
Greatest vintages still drinking well: '88, '90, '91, '92, '93
Retail price: $28
Winemaker: Tod Dexter

FULL FLAVOURED DRY WHITES

*Tarrawarra Chardonnay (Yarra Valley) BM

A very classy, elegant Chardonnay that typically exhibits good depth of fruit wrapped up in a "tight" structure, and with the flavour complexity that can only come from the employment of the best Burgundian winemaking techniques.

Aging potential: 4-8 years
Greatest vintages still drinking well: '88, '90, '91, '92, '94
Retail price: $27
Winemaker: Martin Williams

*Tyrrell's Old Winery Chardonnay (Sth Eastern Australia) V

Some terrific value wines have been released under this label in recent years. This wine is typically full of juicy Chardonnay flavours intertwined with smoky, bacon-like oak.

Aging potential: A drink now style that is best enjoyed over the first few years after release.
Greatest vintages still drinking well: '92, '93, '94 '95
Retail price: $14
Winemaker: Andrew Spinnaze

*Tyrrell's Vat 47 Pinot Chardonnay (Lower Hunter Valley) BM

Typically a restrained Chardonnay that exhibits refined fruit characteristics of peach and citrus along with a long sappy finish that is one of this wine's trademarks. The oak is characteristically well handled and manifests itself as a whisper of spicy, vanillin and cedar in the background.

Aging potential: A wine that ages very well, even the lesser years needs 5 years+, and most vintages will live and develop positively for 8-12 years+
Greatest vintages still drinking well: '88, '90, '91, '92, '93, '94
Retail price: $29
Winemaker: Andrew Spinnaze

Wyangan Estate Chardonnay (Griffith & Eden Valley) V

The Wyangan Estate Chardonnays are typically rich, broadly flavoured wines oozing ripe Chardonnay aromas and flavours (peaches, apricots and melon) and substantial toast/vanillin oak. For those seeking flavoursome Chardonnay, this wine represents terrific value.

Aging potential: 2-4 years
Greatest vintages still drinking well: '91, '92, '93, '94, '95
Winemaker's food match: Generally best served with white meats, veal or with soft cheeses.
Retail price: $13
Winemaker: Shayne Cunningham

Technical data: Some cool climate Semillon is included in the blend in some vintages. This lends the wine a slight herbaceous character. Grapes for this wine are generally machine harvested at night to utilise the cooler temperatures. Only free-run juice is used; it is cold settled, inoculated with a yeast culture and barrel fermented. Barrel fermentation takes place in new American oak barriques (medium toast) and aged on lees for a minimum of 6 months. The wine is then racked out of the barrels, stabilised and bottle aged a further 3-6 months prior to release.

Yalumba Family Reserve Chardonnay (Barossa Valley) V

This wine has undergone a worthy change of style with the '94 vintage with more emphasis on fruit and less on oak. A soft fleshy wine that exhibits ripe melon and tropical fruit flavours and aromas along with nutty, vanillin oak.

Aging potential: Made for early drinking, 2-3 years
Greatest vintages still drinking well: '92, '93, '94
Winemaker's food match: This wine will best compliment white meat dishes and most Asian dishes except those that are heavily spiced
Retail price: $12
Winemaker: Alan Hoey

Technical data: The wine undergoes maturation on lees as well as 2 months of oak maturation in barrels at least 1 year or older.

Yarra Ridge Chardonnay (Yarra Valley) V

Typically exhibits rich aromas of tropical fruit, peach and melon, a full flavoured palate with well integrated vanillin oak lingering on the dry finish. Yarra Ridge vineyards was recently purchased by Mildara Blass which may or may not herald a change in style and/or quality for this label. As yet it is too early to tell.

Aging potential: 2-4 years
Greatest vintages: '91, '92, '93
Winemaker's food match: Chicken, fish, pasta
Retail price: $16
Winemaker: Louis Bialkower and Rob Dolan

Other Recommended Producers of Chardonnay: Barwang, Bridgewater Mill, Dalwhinnie, De Bortoli Yarra Valley, Diamond Valley, Freycinet, Geoff Weaver Stafford Ridge, Heggies, Hillstowe, Lindemans Padthaway, Massoni, Petersons, Pooles Rock, Rothbury, Salitage, St Huberts, Wignalls, amongst others

Recommended Producers of Others Styles: Evans & Tate Sauvignon Blanc, Fermoy Estate Semillon, Mount Avoca Semillon, amongst others

SWEET & STICKY - THE DESSERT WINES

The title above, although appropriate, is misleading on two counts. Firstly, even though they are undoubtably sweet, the very best "stickies" show clean acid and this with the help of the unique spicy character of botrytis helps stop these wines from becoming cloying in the mouth. Secondly the title "dessert wine" seems to suggest that these wines are only suitable to drink with dessert. Stickies are in fact equally enjoyable with pate or strongly flavoured cheeses, especially a 'blue'. They are also delicious when matched simply, with a fruit plate.

LEGEND OF SYMBOLS

"**BM**" - stands for bench-mark. Wines titles that are followed by this symbol are wines to measure others by.

"**preBM**" - indicates a wine that has shown itself capable of producing wines of a BM standard however the 'label' lacks either a long enough history of vintages or perhaps the consistency to be titled as such.

"**V**" - stands for Value. These wines represent very good examples of their region and/or wine style, and are relatively inexpensive (at least under $20).

"*****" - the author has compiled this wine description with little if any feed-back from the producer.

*Cranswick Estate (Riverina) preBM

A very refined sticky that typically exhibits high class vanillin, toasty oak characters and rich apricot fruit. Vibrant acidity and perfect balance ensure a lightness on the palate that belies the wine's power. The wines released have so far been of BM quality and future consistency will warrant such a rating.

Aging potential: 7-10 years+
Great vintages still drinking well: '93, '94, '95
Retail price: $22 (375 ml)
Winemaker: Ian Hongell

De Bortoli Noble One Semillon (Riverina) BM

A full bodied, ultra-rich sticky. Typically jam-packed with viscous honey, apricot and cumquat flavours complemented by very subtle toasted vanillin characters of fine French oak and a firm backbone of acid. This luscious, decadently rich wine remains the benchmark for Australian botrytised Semillon.

Aging potential: the characteristics of the wine will change but the wine should last for at least 40 years.
Greatest vintages: '82, '84, '87, '90, '93
Winemaker's food match: Fresh fruit or desserts based on fresh fruit.
Retail price: $19 (375ml) & $38 (750ml)
Winemaker: Darren De Bortoli

Technical data: Botrytis occurs naturally in the Riverina. Factors which can affect the style include the level and 'cleanness' of botrytis infection. In other words, it is important that there aren't other undesirable moulds present. An important characteristic of Semillon is that it is a thin skinned variety susceptible to Noble Rot infection. This wine is matured in 100% fully imported French Oak barriques. The wood comes from the heart of the tree and therefore is tightly grained otherwise leakage due to capillary action from the high sugar content of this wine will occur. The favoured cooperage is Seguin Moreau.

Gramps Botrytis Semillon (Riverina/Cowra) V

A middleweight in terms of richness, this wine typically exhibits sweet apricot and citrus flavours along with cleansing acid on the finish.

Aging potential: 2-4 years
Greatest vintages: '90
Winemaker's food match: Excellent with fruit tarts, soft cheeses, fruit and nuts.
Retail price: $12 (375ml)
Winemaker: Philip Laffer

*Grosset Noble Riesling (Clare Valley) BM

Typically exhibits intense, luscious Riesling (lemon/lime) characters, subtle botrytis and electric acidity that balances the natural sweetness of the wine and gives it a clean, fresh finish. A contrast to the fully blown, super-sweet style of sticky, this wine, like all the wines of this producer, is bottled elegance.

Aging potential: 5 - 8 years
Greatest vintages still drinking well: (In order) '95, '94, '91
Retail price: $18 (375ml)
Winemaker: Jeffrey Grosset

Hardy's Collection Beerenauslese Riesling BM

A difficult to find wine that is much sought after by 'sticky' enthusiasts. Typically shows a good balance of all components with apricot and honey richness, lemon/lime varietal characteristics and vibrant acidity.

Aging potential: probably best drunk young between 3 - 5 years of age however the better vintages such as those listed below will live, and develop for many years more.
Greatest vintages still drinking well: '85, '87, '92, '94
Retail price: $22 (375ml)
Winemaker: Tom Newton

Heggies Botrytis Riesling (Eden Valley) V

Typically shows a good balance of lemon/lime fruit, orange peel botrytis characters, sweet residual sugar and acid. When young this wine has obvious varietal intensity and botrytis character. With age, the palate gains greater richness, and exhibits more honey, apricot characters yet the finish remains clean with crisp acidity.

Aging potential: 8-10 years. The recent wines of '92 and '94 have great aging potential, more so than previous releases.
Greatest vintages still drinking well: '92, '94
Retail price: $14 (375m)
Winemaker: Simon Adams

Technical data: This wine undergoes no oak treatment. In the vineyard, fig canopies are encouraged to create the higher humidity necessary for botrytis development. In the winery, the wine undergoes total juice oxidation in order to precipitate potential browning compounds that would normally develop with time. Hence the aging potential of '92 and '94 compared to previous releases.

*Henschke Noble Rot Riesling (Eden Valley) preBM

This wine is typically complex, often exhibiting a wide variety of flavours and aromas such as: apricot nectar, baked quince and orange peel botrytis. The palate is rich and luscious yet well balanced by crisp acidity.

Aging potential: 7-10 years+
Greatest vintages still drinking well: '84, '87, '90, '92 (No wine has been produced since '92 as vintage conditions have not been favourable to the development of botrytis).
Winemaker's food match: Best with fresh fruit desserts, such as cherries mangoes, pears, berry fruits and cream or with soft cheeses
Retail price: $18 (375ml)
Winemaker: Stephen Henschke

Miranda Estate Golden Botrytis (Riverina/King Valley) preBM

Only one vintage of this wine has been released yet it is impressive enough to merit a listing. It is a luscious, honeyed wine that combines the rich apricot, fig and pear characteristics of ultra ripe Semillon with the citrus-like, passionfruit cut of Riesling. There is plenty of marmalade-like botrytis as well as some subtle, toffee development.

Aging potential: 4-10 years+
Greatest vintages still drinking well: '93 (1st vintage)
Retail price: $18 (375ml)
Winemaker: Shayne Cunningham

Technical data: This wine is a blend of 65% Semillon sourced from the Riverina region of NSW and 35% Riesling from Guy Darling's Koombahla vineyard in King Valley.

Peter Lehmann Noble Semillon (Barossa Valley) V

Typically a luscious and complex sweet, white table wine which, whilst being very sweet, is not cloying on the palate. Often described as having rich apricot overtones, with fig and honey not far behind.

Aging potential: 10 years plus
Greatest vintages: '82, '84, '87, '92
Winemaker's food match: Serve lightly chilled as an accompaniment to pate, cheese and fresh fruits, or with desserts.
Retail price: $13 (375ml)
Winemaker: Peter Lehmann, Andrew Wigan, Peter Scholz and Leonie Lange.

Technical data: Over 15 years intensive study of potential vineyard locations capable of developing botrytis in favourable seasonal conditions has allowed the winemaking team to identify the vineyards from which it can source premium botrytis affected Semillon. In these sites, botrytis infection occurs naturally in the late Autumn. This wine is only made in years when it is deemed that the level of infection is up to scratch. Fermentation and subsequent maturation in new oak adds complexity without dominating the whole.

*Seville Estate Botrytis affected Riesling (Yarra Valley) BM
[previously titled Beerenauslese or Trockenbeerenauslese]

Searingly rich and luscious Riesling with viscous mouthfeel and spicy acid.

Aging potential: 7-10 years+
Greatest vintages: '80, '81, '82, '84, '85, '87, '91, '92, '93
Retail price: $ 30 (375ml)
Winemaker: Peter McMahon

*Tim Knappstein Botrytis Riesling (Clare Valley) BM

Extremely difficult to find wine due to its small production and its cult-like status amongst wine enthusiasts. Intense limey, Riesling characters are enhanced by spicy, orange zest botrytis and lively acidity. Typically exhibits wonderful balance and a delicacy that is rare in Australian dessert styles.

Aging potential: 3-6 years
Greatest vintages: '80, '81, '84, '86, '89, '92
Retail price: $15 (375ml)
Winemaker: Andrew Hardy

Technical data: Formerly labelled as "Auslese, Beerenauslese, or Trockenbeerenauslese, this wine is only produced when the vintage conditions are ideal for the formation of the botrytis mould. Unfortunately the last time such conditions arose was for the '92 vintage.

Tollana Botrytis Riesling (Coonawarra, Eden Valley) V

The wine typically exhibits a complex bouquet of noble rot characters (orange peel and dried apricots). The palate is luscious and shows rich honey and raisin flavours. Although very sweet, this wine characteristically has enough acidity to prevent it from being cloying in the mouth.

Aging potential: 6-12 years
Greatest vintages still drinking well: '87, '91, '93
Winemaker's food match: Crisp, high acid desserts such as sorbet or fruit based desserts.
Retail price: $12
Winemaker: Neville Falkenberg

Technical data: 90% of the Riesling grapes used to make this wine are sourced from Coonawarra. Around 10% Eden Valley Traminer is used in the final blend. Some cane cutting is used in the vineyard to enhance the shrivelling of the berries and maximise flavour.

Yarra Ridge Botrytis Semillon (Riverina) preBM

Typically a rich, golden colour with the aromas of honeysuckle, figs and apricots, which combine with a unctuous palate of honey, toffee and marmalade flavours.

Aging potential: 5 years
Greatest vintages still drinking well: '93
Winemaker's food match: Blue cheese, fruits, simple desserts (not too much cream and definitely not chocolate)
Retail price: $22 (375ml)
Winemaker: Louis Bialkower, Rob Dolan.

Technical data: Produced from grapes grown in the Griffith/Riverina area, Australia's prime source of this luscious wine style. This wine is whole bunch pressed over a minimum of 30 hours. The juices are macerated back over the berries during this process with the result being a richer, more luscious wine. The wine is barrel fermented for 20 weeks at 15°.

*Wilton Estate Botrytis Semillon (Riverina) preBM

A luscious wine that is fast establishing itself as a challenger to De Bortoli's "Noble One". Typically a concentrated, honeyed wine with apricot and fig characteristics along with orange zest botrytis. Searingly sweet sugar levels make this a wine for the 'super sticky' lovers.

Aging potential: 3-6 years
Greatest vintages still drinking well: '90, '91, '92
Retail price: $23 (375ml) $40 (750ml)
Winemaker: Adrian Sheridan

Other Recommended Producers of sweet & sticky styles: Brown Bothers, Crawford River, D'Arenberg, McWilliams, Primo Estate, Vasse Felix, Amongst others

TOKAYS AND MUSCATS

Australia's most undervalued wines. The value here is probably due to the wide public misconception that Tokays & Muscats are similar to ports. Yes, they are fortified wines, and yes, they are packaged in the same way, but they are most definitely not, ports. They are in fact sweet viscous dessert wines of the highest merit. The raisiny, chocolaty Muscats taste, literally, like liquid Christmas pudding and the more complex Tokays are blessed with the distinctive flavours of toffee and sweet, cold tea amongst other characteristics. These sublime wines are unique to Australia, and I have a sneaking suspicion that they will be the next "big thing" in the U.K. market where the climate is perhaps more suited to their higher alcohol.

Note: for those who find these wines too rich, don't worry what the snobs say, simply keep a bottle in the fridge and serve it chilled. Alternatively, pour an innexpensive example over ice cream and preserved fruits. Delicious!

LEGEND OF SYMBOLS

"BM" - stands for bench-mark. Wines titles that are followed by this symbol are wines to measure others by.

"preBM" - indicates a wine that has shown itself capable of achieving a BM standard however the 'label' lacks either a long enough history of vintages or perhaps the consistency to be titled as such.

"V" - stands for Value. These wines represent very good examples of their region and/or wine style, and are relatively inexpensive (at least under $20).

"*" - the author has compiled this wine description with little if any feed-back from the producer.

ALL SAINTS
The Lyrebird range V

BAILEYS
"Warby Range" V
"Founder Series" preBM
"Winemakers Selection" BM
"Gold Label" Muscat BM

CAMPBELLS
Liqueur Muscat and Tokay V
"Merchant Prince" Rutherglen Muscat BM

CHAMBERS ROSEWOOD
Special Liqueur Tokay & Muscat V
Old Liqueur Muscat and Old Liqueur Tokay BM

LINDEMANS
White Label Muscat Solera 1625 BM
Tokay Solera WH2 BM

MORRIS
Morris Liqueur Muscat and Tokay V
Old Premium Liqueur Muscat and Tokay BM

SEPPELT
Show Muscat and Show Tokay BM

Other Recommended Producers; Bullers Amongst others.

SPARKLING WINES

This collection of wines vary considerably in weight of flavour and style. A number of factors contribute to this variation: What grape varieties were used to make the base wine, and, if it is a Pinot\Chardonnay blend (now typical of premium Australian fizz), is it Chardonnay dominant or Pinot (Noir) dominant? From which regions where the grapes sourced? Was the wine bottle fermented and if so, how long was it matured on yeast lees? How heavily has it been liqueured? (See glossary) All these as well as other factors will influence the finished wine. Despite these production, and therefore style, differences, I have decided not to split these wines up under separate categories for the sake of both simplicity and my sanity. You will therefore need to read the wine descriptions carefully. I can say, however, that all of the wines listed here are dry styles, with the exception of the Sparkling Burgundies which traditionally have a hint of sweetness.

LEGEND OF SYMBOLS

"BM" - stands for bench-mark. Wines titles that are followed by this symbol are wines to measure others by.
"preBM" - indicates a wine that has shown itself capable of producing wines of a BM standard however the 'label' lacks either a long enough history of vintages or perhaps the consistency to be titled as such.
"V" - stands for Value. These wines represent very good examples of their region and/or wine style, and are relatively inexpensive (at least under $20).
"*" - the author has compiled this wine description with little if any feed-back from the producer.

*Andrew Garrett Pinot Noir Chardonnay N.V.

Typically a soft creamy wine that typically exhibits berry fruit flavours and a pale salmon hue. Very good value.

Aging potential: Drink now
Greatest vintages still drinking well: Non Vintage
Retail price: $14
Winemaker: Phil Rescke

Angus Brut

(see Yalumba)

*Cope-Williams "Romsey" (Macedon) BM

A richly flavoured, complex wine, typical of the sparkling wines of this region, with bready, yeasty, nutty characters that linger on the breath.

Aging potential: Drink now
Greatest vintages still drinking well: Non Vintage
Retail price: $30
Winemaker: Michael Cope-Williams

Croser (Piccadilly Valley, Adelaide Hills) BM

One of Australia's most refined and tightly structured sparkling wines characteristically exhibiting subtle but intense fruit flavours, clean acidity, and a creamy, persistent bead.

Aging potential: 2-4 years (considerably longer when released as a late disgorged wine)
Greatest vintages still drinking well: '90, '92, '88, '87, '91 (Croser's order)
Retail price: $33
Winemaker: Brian Croser

Technical data: Hand picked Piccadilly Valley Pinot Noir and Chardonnay grapes are chilled and pressed as whole bunches. Only the heart run juice (1st pressing) is used to produce Croser and no additives are used in the winemaking process. Croser matures on yeast lees for two years before remuage and disgorging. It is a vintage wine.

Domaine Chandon Vintage Brut BM

A harmonious and complex wine that typically exhibits an array of flavours (citrus, apple, spice, nuts, bread). The wine has a fine, creamy mousse, good weight of flavour and a soft, dry finish.

Aging potential: Although these wine drink well when young and fresh, the age gracefully for between 5-10 years developing into fuller styles with quite powerful aromas.
Greatest vintages still drinking well: '86, '90, '91, '92, '93
Retail price: $30
Winemaker: Dr Tony Jordan, Wayne Donaldson assisted by Maryann Egan and Ken Heally

Technical data: Blended from between 30 and 50 base wines produced from grapes grown in 16 cool climate vineyards in Victoria, South Australia and Tasmania. (Hence the complexity of flavours). Made from Chardonnay, Pinot Noir (roughly equal proportions) and a little (1 or 2%) Pinot Meunier. Spends between 2.5 - 5 years on lees prior to disgorgement. A proportion of the base wine undergoes malo-lactic fermentation (20% in the '92 for example).

Domain Chandon Blanc de Blancs BM

A wine that typically shows delicious yeast\aged Chardonnay flavours and aromas (creme caramel, oatmeal, toast, roasted almonds). The wine has a creamy mousse (bubbles) and a full, round palate that finishes refreshingly dry.

Aging potential: 5-10 years, the '86 is still drinking beautifully.
Greatest vintages still drinking well: '90, '92
Retail price: $30
Winemaker: Dr Tony Jordan, Wayne Donaldson assisted by Maryann Egan and Ken Heally

Technical data: 100% Chardonnay. See Brut data.

Domaine Chandon Blanc de Noirs preBM

A full flavoured wine that typically exhibits delicious Pinot characteristics (red currants, pencil shavings, bread\dough, and savoury, nuances), good richness and lingering flavour.

Aging potential: 5-10 years
Winemaker's food match: An excellent "food wine" compatible with a range of food types from oysters to spicy Asian dishes.
Greatest vintages still drinking well: '90
Retail price: $30
Winemaker: Wayne Donaldson, Tony Jordan assisted by Maryann Egan and Ken Heally

Technical data: As for Brut except 100% Pinot Noir

Fleur de Lys Premium Cuvee

(See Seppelt)

*Hanging Rock "Macedon" BM

Another rich and complex example of what this region is capable of producing. Typically powerful with a full flavoured, well structured palate, creamy bead and a lingering, doughy finish. Perhaps Australia's finest bubbly.

Aging potential: 2-4 years
Greatest vintages still drinking well: Non Vintage
Retail price: $35
Winemaker: John Ellis

*Jansz Cuvee Brut (Pipers, Tasmania) BM

Typically a zesty, citrus-like fizz with nutty yeast characters. Very classy.

Aging potential: 2-6 years
Greatest vintages still drinking well: Non Vintage
Retail price: $30
Winemaker: Gary Ford

*Killawarra Premier Vintange Brut "V"

Quite a richly flavoured style, with toast and citrus characters and a rounded mouthfeel.

Aging potential: Drink now
Greatest vintages still drinking well: '92, '93
Retail price: $13
Winemaker: Peter Gago

Petaluma "Croser"

(see "Croser")

Peter Rumball Sparkling Shiraz (Coonawarra) BM

This is a rich, fruit driven style with a long elegant palate, soft tannin and a delicate sweetness. One of the best examples of this wine genre.

Aging potential: Drinks well on release yet will benefit from around 5 years bottle age.
Greatest vintages still drinking well: Non Vintage
Winemaker's food match: Strongly flavoured meats such as turkey, duck, buffalo, kangaroo, or goat. Cheeses such as Stilton or other blue-veins, King Island cheddar cheeses
Desserts such as: Blackberry, blueberry tarts, plum pudding.
Retail price: $22
Winemaker: Peter Rumball

Technical data: 100% Shiraz is used. The Shiraz pressings can be added back into the wine to give a very big fruit base. The wine is given a reasonable amount of oak treatment. The liquering (added at disgorgement) plays an extremely important role. The liqueur balances the wine, adding sweetness and complexity. It exerts as much influence on the finished wine as the grape variety and region and for this reason Peter Rumball has conducted a great deal of experimentation to get his liqueur just right.

*Rockford Black Shiraz (Barossa Valley) BM

It is very difficult to get your hands on a bottle of this cult wine, yet you will only need one sip to justify your efforts. Typically rich and round with the aromas and flavours of berries, plums, and spice along with chocolate and earth complexity and the faintest trace of aniseed. A slightly sweet, lingering finish is also the norm. Wonderful, complex drinking.

Aging potential: 10 years + (Drinks deliciously on release however those who cellar this wine for at least 3-5 years will be amply rewarded for their self discipline)
Greatest vintages still drinking well: Non Vintage
Ex Winery price: $35
Winemaker: Robert O'Callaghan

*Seaview Pinot Noir Chardonnay Vintage V

The last two vintages of this wine have made been of preBM quality and further consistency will merit such a rating. Outstanding value with good depth of peachy, citrus-like fruit and toasty, yeast characters.

Aging potential: 1-3 years
Greatest vintages still drinking well: '90, '91, '92, '93, '94
Retail price: $14
Winemaker: Ed Carr

Seppelt Fleur de Lys Premium Cuvee V

This wine features attractive citrus-like fruit combined with creamy yeast characters. It shows an excellent depth & persistence of flavour balanced by crisp, drying acidity.

Aging potential: Made for immediate enjoyment.
Greatest vintages still drinking well: Non Vintage
Winemaker's food match: An aperitif style that can go with subtly flavoured dishes.
Retail price: $13
Winemaker: Ian McKenzie

Technical data: This wine is blended from several vintages of base wines (1-5 years old) that are sourced from five regions in South Australia and Victoria and is bottle fermented.

Seppelt Harper's Range Sparkling Burgundy preBM

Ripe rich, flavoursome Shiraz characteristics (plums, berries, earth, spice) along with subtle oak can be expected here. The wine's inherent sweetness is balanced by soft, drying tannins and clean acidity.

Aging potential: 2-5 years
Greatest vintages still drinking well: '63, '72, '82, '85, '86, '91 (Great Western releases), '92.
Winemaker's food match: Turkey, game bird, cheese and light fruit desserts.
Retail price: $17
Winemaker: Ian McKenzie

Seppelt "Show" Sparkling Burgundy (Great Western) BM

Typically a complex and full flavoured wine. The palate has ripe, spicy, sweet plummy fruit with rich chocolaty maturation characters and hints of earth. A soft and rich wine that finishes dry with lingering flavours.

Aging potential: Released at 10 years of age (2-5 years on cork) and will live for fifty years.
Greatest vintages still drinking well: '44, '64, '68, '85, '86, '87, '90, '91
Winemaker's food match: Christmas turkey, or plum pudding
Retail price: $36
Winemaker: Ian McKenzie

Technical data: 100% Great Western from the "St Peter's" vineyard (out the front of the winery) The vines in this unirrigated, vineyard are 50 years+ of age and extremely low yielding (1.5 tonne\acre). The wine spends 12 months in 100% old oak vats (very little oak character) and 8 years on lees before disgorgement.

Seppelt "Salinger" BM

This wine characteristically displays an elegant bouquet of uplifted Chardonnay (citrus, nuts) fruit combined with yeast complexity derived from both fermentation and extended bottle maturation on yeast lees. The wine has mouth filling flavour that lingers and finishes dry with crisp acidity.

Aging potential: 3 years.
Greatest vintages still drinking well: '84, '88, '89, '90, '92, '93, '94
Winemaker's food match: Aperitif or food wine.
Retail price: $30
Winemaker: Ian McKenzie

Technical data: A blend of Chardonnay (predominant), Pinot Noir and some Pinot Meunier sourced from cool-cold climate vineyards in NSW (Tumbarumba), Victoria (Drumborg, Strathbogies), and SA (Adelaide Hills). Very little oak is used if at all. The base wine does not undergo any malo-lactic fermentation so as to keep the fruit flavours as fresh as possible and retain natural acidity. After a long, slow, secondary fermentation in the bottle, the wine is aged for 3 years+ on yeast lees.

Taltarni Brut Tache V

Pale salmon in colour this wine typically shows a creamy mouthfeel with attractive citrus and strawberry fruit flavours. There is a hint of sweetness on the finish which allows the wine to be served well chilled.

Aging potential: This is a Non Vintage wine made for immediate consumption.
Greatest vintages still drinking well: Non Vintage
Retail price: $15
Winemaker: Dominique Portet and Greg Gallagher

Technical data: This wine is made by the traditional Methode Champenoise. It spends 12 months on lees and its colour is derived by an addition of a small quantity of red wine (Malbec) at disgorgement time. Whilst being predominantly Chardonnay and Pinot Noir this wine does contain a small amount of Pinot Meunier (the third variety of Champagne) and Chenin Blanc. A small percentage of the Chardonnay is sourced from Taltarni"s Tasmanian vineyards and 5% of the blend is Reserve wine (older wine).

Yalumba Angus Brut V

Always tremendous value. Made predominantly from Semillon this wine typically exhibits lemony, citrus flavours, toasty complexity and crisp acidity.
Aging potential: This is a non-vintage wine and as such is best drunk young.
Greatest vintages still drinking well: Non Vintage
Winemaker's food match: An aperitif style although its depth of flavour will support seafood and white meat dishes.
Retail price: $7
Winemaker: Geoff Linton, Louisa Rose

Technical data: A multi regional blend with the most significant component being Semillon grown in the Barossa and SA Riverland. There is also a significant proportion of Pinot Noir. The grapes are picked early to retain good acid. The wine undergoes malo-lactic fermentation to enhance the softness of the wine.

Yalumba Angus Brut Rose V

Terrific value, this wine exhibits lifted berry/strawberry aromas, leading to a creamy palate with subtle toast and yeast nuances. The finish is clean with crisp acidity.

Aging potential: This is a non-vintage wine and as such is best drunk young.
Greatest vintages still drinking well: Non Vintage
Winemaker's food match: see above listing.
Retail price: $7
Winemaker: Geoff Linton, Louisa Rose.

Technical data: The wine is a multi regional blend with the most significant component being Cabernet Sauvignon grown in the Riverland of SA For winemaking see listing above.

Yalumba Cuvee One Prestige V

A full flavoured style with crisp lemon tartness overlying a creamy textured palate. Subtle nuances of Pinot Noir (strawberry) and Chardonnay (nuttiness) are typical along with a hint of yeasty character.

Aging potential: The wine should be consumed within twelve months of disgorgement, ensuring that the fruit and yeast characters are primary (aging will produce toasty flavours that dominate the fruit).
Greatest vintages still drinking well: Non Vintage
Winemaker's food match: An aperitif style whose depth of flavour will also support seafood and white meat dishes.
Retail price: $15
Winemaker: Geoff Linton, Louisa Rose

Continued on facing page...

Continued...

Technical data: Made from the traditional French Champagne varieties: Pinot Noir (65%) & Chardonnay (35%) this wine spends a minimum of two years en tirage before being disgorged and liquered to 8g/l sugar. A multi regional wine, with components drawn from many of Australia's coolest regions such as the Eden Valley, Adelaide Hills, Yarra Valley, Coonawarra, King Valley etc. A minor percentage of the wine undergoes malo-lactic fermentation.

Yalumba "D" BM

An elegant yet complex and flavourful wine with layers of flavour exhibiting subtle characters ranging from anise and berry (Pinot Noir characters) to nutty and grapefruit (Chardonnay characters) through to the toasty, slightly cheesy aromas derived from maturation on yeast, in the bottle (en tirage) for several years. The palate is long and the wine's inherent richness is balanced by citrus-like acidity.

Aging potential: Best within 12 months of disgorgement as prolonged bottle age promotes the development of toasty flavours that over power the more delicate fruit and yeast derived characters.

Greatest vintages still drinking well: '88, '90, '92

Winemaker's food match: Great as aperitif and works as an accompaniment to hors d'oeuvres and finger foods. However its complexity of flavour provides for its matching with lightly flavoured foods such as seafood, poultry, light meats and cheeses.

Retail price: $27

Winemaker: Geoff Linton, Louisa Rose.

Technical data: Made from grapes grown entirely in the cool climate viticultural areas of Australia. Typically a blend of 65% Pinot Noir, 30% Chardonnay and 5% Pinot Meunier. 100% of the wine undergoes malo-lactic fermentation. Oak barrels are used to make and mature the "reserve" wine (which makes up around 15% of the finished blend) Oak flavours are not sought therefore old barrels (4 years plus) are utilised.

Other Recommended Producers: Hollick Cornell (white & red), Irvine, Jim Barry (Sparkling Red), Joseph Sparkling Red, Padthaway Estate, Penley Estate, Mountadam, Redbank, Amongst others

Glossary

GLOSSARY

An extensive listing of wine making and tasting terms used both in this guide and throughout wine literature.

Acetic Acid
See volatile acidity

Acid
The crisp, zesty lift that acid lends a wine is essential to its enjoyment and structure. Acids, mostly Tartaric, Malic, and Citric, play an important role in a wine's brilliance of colour, in "lifting" the aroma, and also in the mouthfeel. The role of acid on the palate of a wine is to balance the fruit richness (or sugar richness in the case of sweet wines), to give it a vibrancy, and a clean, dry finish. It helps to preserve the wine and also works as a natural antibacterial agent. Wines with an excess of acid (especially Malic) tend to taste hard or sour on the finish. Wines that lack acidity, i.e. have a pH that is too high, will tend to taste flat and have a dull appearance.

Alcohol
A natural by-product of the fermentation process, alcohol is formed, along with carbon dioxide, as a result of yeast's interaction with sugar. The riper the grapes are when harvested (and consequently the higher their sugar levels), the higher their potential for alcohol. There are, however, a number of occurrences in the winery that can affect the final alcohol level of a given wine. Fermentation can be stopped prematurely by the addition of sulphur to the fermenting wine, by adding alcohol (as in fortified wines), or via a fine filtration. All these procedures will end fermentation prematurely, leaving a trace of residual sugar (and hence potential alcohol) in the wine. In a well balanced wine, the alcohol content will be almost imperceptible to taster. Typically, alcohol lends a certain sweetness and roundness to a wine and, when out of balance, manifests itself as an obvious hotness on the finish.

Aroma
Amongst some wine professionals, this term is used to identify the scents associated with young wines, as opposed to the complex bouquet that develops with bottle age. However, in much wine literature, this book included, the two terms are used synonymously to mean the fragrance of a given wine.

Astringent
Drying mouth puckering effect of high levels of tannin and acidity in the wine. Acceptable in moderate levels and desired in young, full bodied reds where the tannin content (resulting from extended maceration and oak aging) acts as a natural preservative in the wine. Astringency will generally soften with bottle age.

Austere
A term used to describe wines that exhibit a certain restraint of flavour. Such wines show a subtlety in the mouth that is closely linked to balance and bodes well for the longevity of the wine. Most commonly observed in cool climate Cabernet Sauvignon, Hunter Valley Semillon, and other whites with firm acidity.

Balanced
A term used to describe a wine that has all of its characteristics: fruit, acid, alcohol, tannin, and oak, in equilibrium. It follows then that wines described as 'out of balance' will have at least one of these characteristics sticking out like a sore thumb.

Barrel Fermentation
Process whereby the wine is fermented in small oak barrels rather than larger vats or in stainless steel. Most commonly associated with white wine production, especially Chardonnay, although some of Australia's better reds, most famously Penfolds Grange, undergo partial barrel fermentation. Barrel fermentation encourages a better integration of oak flavour, and white wines that undergo this process tend to show less overt 'fruity' characters. This is because barrel fermentation is less likely to be temperature controlled and therefore occurs at a relatively high temperature. This "hot" ferment burns off the esters that are responsible for aromatic characters in wines.

Barrique
The traditional oak barrel of Bordeaux, the barrique holds 225 litres of wine and is widely used in the production of premium Australian wines.

Battonage
A French wine making term used to denote the practice of lees stirring. This process has a softening effect on the wine as well adding an extra element of flavour complexity.

Baumé
Measurement of the sugar level, and hence potential alcohol, in grape juice prior to fermentation. One degree baumé roughly equates to 1% of potential alcohol.

Beerenauslese
Very sweet German white wine made from extremely ripe grapes often affected by botrytis. Used on Australian wine labels to denote a similarly sweet wine and it will no doubt continue to be used until an original scale of sweetness is devised.

Body
No simple definition here as "body" is often equated with different elements of a wine's composition. Alcohol strength, tannin, richness of flavour, either of these, or a combination of all of them, can all be used to classify a wine as full, medium or light bodied. In regards to this book, and perhaps the majority of wine journalism, the term 'body' is, in the case of red wines, synonymous with weight of alcohol, tannin, and flavour- all taken into consideration. In regard to whites, the term "full bodied" is generally reserved for wood treated wines as these tend to be the richest in flavour.

Botrytis
Botrytis cinerea, also known as noble rot, is a fungus that attacks ripe grapes especially in warm, humid conditions. Although feared by producers of dry wines, it is often encouraged by makers of late harvest, dessert styles. In such cases the mould assists the winemaker by helping to shrivel the berries, concentrate the sugar and flavour components of the grape while lending a spicy, orange peel character to the finished wine.

Bouquet
See Aroma

Broad
Wines described as "broad" show a richness of fruit that tends to overpower the acid in the wine. Such wines have a soft and somewhat oily texture in the mouth.

Brut
Used on sparkling wines to indicate a wine that is relatively dry, i.e., has not been liqueured too heavily.

Carbonic Maceration
Fermentation technique in which uncrushed, whole bunches of grapes ferment in an oxygen free environment. This technique tends to produce light, soft and fruity reds and is most famously utilised in the Beaujolais region in France. Can also be a feature of premium Pinot Noir wines, both in France and the 'new world', where whole bunches included in the ferment means that a percentage of the wine has undergone CM.

Cedar
A resinous, aromatic characteristic bestowed on the wine by contact with new oak. A very attractive aroma that is literally reminiscent of cedar wood, and is most commonly associated with French oak and Cabernet Sauvignon wines

Chaptelisation
The practice of raising the potential alcohol of a given wine by the addition of sugar, grape juice, or grape juice concentrate.

Clean
A wine that shows no technical or bacterial faults - no pongy characters.

Corked
A bacterial infection carried by the cork that taints the wine. Tends to manifest itself as a mouldy, wet hession aroma (also likened to damp sawdust) and a bitter stale character dulling the fruit flavour.

Decant
To carefully pour, in one continuous stream, a bottle of wine into another vessel (decanter). With mature red wines, this serves to drain the clear wine away from the sediment that is the natural result of the aging process. With younger, full bodied red wines it is sometimes practiced to help the wine 'open-up' (show all of its fruit character). Directions on how to properly decant a wine are given on page 16.

Extract
Generally used in regard to red wines, to denote the colour, flavour and tannin extracted from the grape skins, pips and stalks during the maceration process.

Filtration
Process by which the wine is passed through a filter to remove any lees, leaving behind a brilliantly clear liquid.

Fining
The practice of clarifying a wine by adding a fining agent through the top of the barrel. A substance that is heavier than the wine itself, such as egg whites, forms on top of the wine then makes its way down through the liquid, trapping any lees like a net and dragging them to the bottom of the barrel or vat.

Fino
A very dry, refreshing style of sherry that generally exhibits a nutty tang resulting from the thick film of yeast, flor, which grows on the surface of the wine while it matures in barrel.

Fortified
The name given to wines made with an extra addition of grape alcohol. This dose of alcohol kills off any microorganisms, stops fermentation (leaving a percentage of unfermented sugar) and of-course raises the alcohol level of the wine. Wines made in this way include: ports, sherry, vermouth etc. and they generally weigh in at around 16-18% alcohol.

Fruity
Wines that are rich in fruit flavour. Sometimes incorrectly used to denote wines that exhibit some sugar sweetness. Dry Sauvignon Blanc and Gewurztraminer are fruity, Late harvest, dessert wines are sweet.

Free-Run
The juice that drains from the grapes prior to them being pressed. As most of the harsher elements of wine, such as tannins, are derived from the grape skins, pips and stalks, free-run juice tends to produce softer, more delicately flavoured wines. Especially favoured in the production of high quality sparkling wine.

Gamey
The smell of roasted game meats that is sometimes exhibited by better red wines. When in balance, such a character lends the wine a delicious complexity.

Generic
Wines labeled generically are labeled by their region or style rather than their grape variety. That is, instead of titling a wine as a "Coonawarra Cabernet Sauvignon", you might name it simply "Coonawarra". Of course to do this you would need to control how such a wine was made (and with what grape varieties etc.) so that wine buyers would know what to expect from a "Coonawarra". Such wine making restrictions are extremely problematic in wine producing countries such as Australia where the process of experimentation and exploration is far from over. In the older wine producing countries of Europe, such as France and Italy, most wines are labeled generically. Wines from the French region of Bordeaux for example are named by their sub-region such as Médoc, Graves, Pomerol, generally with no mention of grape variety. In Australia, America, and other parts of the world, there has been a long history of ripping off French generic titling such as Chablis, Burgundy, Hermitage, Champagne, and the like. These French generic titles have been used to label wines that had little if anything in common with those whose names they borrowed, nor even with each other. Thankfully as of 1997 such confusing labeling will cease on Australian wines due to an agreement between Australia and the EEC.

Green
Used to describe wines that have a hard acidic edge associated with excessive Malic acid. The term is also sometimes used in reference to certain red wines, as a synonym for herbaceous. These reds, generally cool climate wines made from Cabernet Sauvignon and/or Merlot, can exhibit green capsicum\ asparagus\ tinned pea\ or grassy characters. It might seem unusual to use a colour to describe a taste or aroma but, apart from the fact that these foods are in fact green, such flavours seem to literally conjure up the colour green in the mind of wine tasters. Interestingly, science is now beginning to vindicate such descriptives via the growing recognition that there does seem to be some transference between the brain centres associated with colour, shape and texture (think of a smooth, roundly flavoured wine), taste, and even sound. Musical wine? Why not.

Hard
Used to describe white wines with excessive acid and reds that have excessive grape tannins that cause the wine to finish with a bitter edge.

Herbaceous
Used to describe both reds and whites that show a character of freshly cut grass\ herbs\ asparagus\ green capsicum (used interchangeably). Mostly associated with Sauvignon Blanc and cool climate Cabernet Sauvignon.

Hogshead
A 300 litre oak barrel that is used for the maturation and, sometimes, the fermentation of wines.

Jammy
The character of very ripe red grapes on the finished wine. Reminiscent of home-made jam.

Lactic Acid
The main acid found in yoghurt and in sour milk, and one of the softer acids that occurs naturally in grapes. In abundance, lends the wine a soft, creamy mouthfeel. See malolactic fermentation.

Late Harvest
Grapes that are left on the vine for extended periods after ripening start to raisin, that is, they start to lose the water component of their juice, thus concentrating the sugar levels. Sweet, dessert style wines that are made from such grapes are sometimes labeled as "Late Harvest". See also Botrytis.

Leathery
The complex aroma of leather is a positive attribute as long as it is not the dominant characteristic of the wine. Often seen in Hunter Valley and McLaren Vale Shiraz, many Italian reds, and high alcohol Australian reds with age.

Lees
Dregs left over in the wine making process, consisting mostly of dead yeast cells along with particles of grape pulp, skin, stalk and stem. Some premium wines, mostly whites that have undergone barrel fermentation, are left on lees (sur lie) and undergo lees stirring. Such lees contact encourages malolactic fermentation and complexity of flavour in the wine. It also tends to encourage a slower absorption, and better integration of, oak characters by the wine in barrel.

Lees Stirring
see Battonage

Long or Length

The after-taste that a wine leaves in your mouth is one of the most important quality indicators. Assuming the finish is in no way bitter or unpleasant, the longer the taste lingers (described as the wine's "length") the better. The length of a wine can also be a good indication of its aging potential i.e.. a long finish (again assuming that the lingering flavours are those of sweet fruit as opposed to hard acid, alcohol, or bitterness) bodes well for the wine's future development, although there are other factors, such as balance and weight, that need to be taken into consideration here.

Maceration

Not to be confused with carbonic maceration. Maceration is a fundamental process in red wine production where the crushed grapes are left in contact with the skins, seeds and stalk particles for an extended period of time. This allows the juice to extract the colour, tannin, and flavour compounds present (primarily in the skin of the grapes). Maceration can be done pre, post and also during fermentation (where the heat of the ferment aids in the extraction process). The juice of all grapes, with a few obscure exceptions, is clear, and therefore, there could be so such a thing as a deeply coloured, red wine without maceration. Modern technology has given us new methods for the extraction of grape skin compounds. One of these is thermovinification which involves the heating of grapes or must prior to fermentation. This process serves to extract colour more speedily and is handy for commercial wines, however, it is not used for fine wine production where maceration remains the preferred process of extraction.

Malic Acid

Along with tartaric acid, Malic acid is one of the most abundant grape acids. It is to be found in nearly all fruits and is at its most overt in green apples where the tart, hard characters of this acid are most apparent. In grapes, Malic acid tends to be most prevalent in unripe berries and breaks down as the grape ripens. In the production of red wines, certain whites, and sparkling wine in general, Malic acid levels are further reduced via malolactic fermentation.

Malolactic Fermentation

A secondary fermentation, occurring after (or more rarely simultaneously to) primary fermentation. Whereas the first fermentation involves yeast at work converting sugar into alcohol, malolactic fermentation involves the work of Lactic bacteria that converts Malic acid into the softer lactic acid. This process not only serves to soften wines with excessive acidity, but also adds an extra dimension of flavour richness.

Must

The mixture of grape juice, pulp, skins, stems fragments, and pips that is the result of grapes that have passed through a crusher. Generally used to refer to this mixture prior to, or during fermentation, after which it is called wine.

Noble Rot
The more traditional and romantic term for botrytis. Australian late harvest wines that have been affected by this fungus are sometimes labeled Noble Semillon or Noble Riesling, depending from which grape variety they have been made.

Nose
The scent of a wine. See Aroma.

Oak
The type of wood used to produce the barrels in which certain styles of wine are fermented and matured. The term "oak" is also used to denote the flavour that such wines receive via their contact with wood. See pg 22.

Oloroso
Richer flavoured, darker coloured sherry. Used on commercial Australian sherry to indicate a sweeter style of sherry.

Oxidised
Wines spoiled by excessive contact with oxygen are described as "oxidised". Oxidation represents a threat to wine quality as soon as grapes are crushed, and perhaps beforehand if there is a high proportion of broken berries. It is most notably a problem with white must where contact with oxygen will cause a browning of the colour and instill unwanted flavour characters (much in the same way as an apple will brown soon after being cut). This problem is overcome via the addition of small amounts of sulphur after crushing and the use of refrigeration in the winery. With certain wine types, most notably fortified wines and Hungarian Tokai, oxidation is encouraged, and with some Chardonnays and certain red wines, gentle, controlled oxidation is used to add complex characters to the wine and increase its aging potential.

pH
The measurement of a wine's hydrogen ion, and therefore acid, concentration. The lower the pH (0-14) the higher the acidity. Neutral liquids such as water and blood have a pH around seven, very strong acids have a pH around zero and a powerful alkali will have a pH of around 14. Acid solutions have a pH less than seven and alkaline solutions have a pH more than seven. Most wines have a pH ranging between three and four. The pH scale is logarithmic, that is, a wine with a pH of three will have ten times the acid level of one with a pH of four.

Press
See wine press.

Pressings
In Australia this term is used on red wine labels to indicate a wine made from a heavier pressing of red grapes (sometimes via a basket press). This more powerful pressing extracts more colour and astringent characters from the grapes and as a result the wine is generally richer and more tannic (see tannin and wine press).

Puncheon
A large oak barrel that holds 450 or 500 litres of wine. The bulky size of such vessels makes them difficult to move, and the increased wine to oak ratio means that little if any oak character is imparted. For these reasons Australian winemakers prefer smaller barrels (such as barriques or hogsheads) when oak character is desired, and stainless steel when it is not. Stainless steel fermentation also has the advantage of temperature control and hence less risk of oxidation and of bacterial spoilage.

Racking
The process of siphoning off the clear wine from the sediment that has settled in the bottom of the wine barrel.

Rancio
A tasting term that is used to describe a highly desirable characteristic of fortified wines that have undergone extended barrel maturation. In Australian wines, it is at its most pronounced in the better Muscats and Tokays (soon to undergo a name change) of North Eastern Victoria. Best described as a rich nutty, burnt butter character that is integrated with the unctuous sweetness and Christmas pudding like complexity of such Muscats and Tokays. Also typical of high quality Port, Cognac, and Madeira.

Residual Sugar
Unfermented sugar present in the finished wine. In moderate quantities, such as those found in many Australian aromatic white wines, residual sugar is not perceived as an overt sweetness by the taster, but rather grants the wine an added richness and viscosity in the mouth.

Sappy
Slightly resinous, grassy character most commonly found in high quality Pinot Noir. I suspect this desirable trait derives from grape stalks that have an impact on these wines due to partial whole bunch fermentation often utilised in their production. Sometimes used to describe the leafy character in cool climate Cabernet Sauvignon or Merlot wines and the resinous character of certain types of oak on young wines.

Solera
A vatting system used in the production of certain fortified wines, most notably sherry. Barrels of wine are stacked on top of each other to form a pyramid. Wine for bottling and sampling is taken from the ground level of the solera and these lower barrels are then topped up from the next layer above them, and this layer is then topped up from the level above it and so on. Any new, younger wine is stacked on top of the solera. This complex and laborious system of blending means that the oldest, on average, more mature wine is always in the lowest barrels and hence in the bottle.

Stalky
see sappy

Structure
The impression of volume or form that a given wine leaves in the mind of an experienced taster. It might seem odd that a liquid should be described in the architectural language of shape but tasters need to make use of such language in an attempt to capture the balance, or lack of it, in any given wine. A red wine that exhibits a balance of all components, when in its prime drinking period, will appear supple and spherical (the mark of such equilibrium). Young tannic reds can seem hard and angular as can whites with high acidity. Sweet wines tend to have a round and heavy mouthfeel although again, if well balanced with lively acidity, will appear deceptively ethereal on the palate. Length of flavour and mouthfeel are both facets of a wine's structure.

Sur Lie
French for "on lees". A winemaking process whereby the wine is left in extended contact with particles of grape pulp, skin, stalk, stem and dead yeast cells. See Lees.

Tannin
An organic substance concentrated in the grape skins, pips, and stalks of the grape. Oak tannins can also be absorbed into a given wine via oak maturation. It is mainly evident in red wines and make its presence known through a chalky dryness in the mouth. Apart from giving the wine this added astringency, tannin functions as a preserving agent. Still unsure? Try chewing on a grape pip.

Tartaric Acid
The most important acid, in terms of wine making, naturally occurring in grapes. Tartaric acid is vital, not only in the flavour of a wine but also in its vibrancy of colour and its role in maintaining this colour with bottle age.

Ullage
The gap of air between the cork and the liquid surface in a bottle of wine is called the ullage. As a given wine ages, the ullage increases. A reasonably high ullage level is a fairly reliable indicator of the soundness of a mature wine. At the very least this indicates that the cork has remained sound. In very old wines, a large ullage is acceptable, and to be expected, as long as it has not dropped below the curved shoulder of the bottle. Ideally speaking, however, the ullage level should remain in the neck of the bottle and some experienced drinkers claim that when a wine's level has reached the base of the neck, it is time to pull the cork.

Vat
A vessel for wine storage and maturation. Sometimes used in Australian wine labeling as in the case of "Tyrrell's Vat 47", where it is simply a brand name.

Varietal
A wine that is titled with the predominant grape variety(ies) from which it has been made. Eg "Chardonnay"

Viscous
The round mouthfeel perceived by the taster especially in regard to sweet wines and, less commonly, richly flavoured wines that have undergone extended barrel maturation.

Vinification
The process of making wines from grapes.

Volatile Acidity
Generally used in reference to acetic acid, although there are a few other acids that are also volatile such as lactic, succinic, amongst others. VA can be beneficial to a wine in small amounts when it is said to lift the aroma and flavour of a wine and lend it a certain complexity. This "lift" is of most benefit to rich and tannic red wines (Penfolds Grange is an example that is often cited) and sweet, late harvest wines rely on a level of VA to balance their unctuous sweetness. In Hungarian Tokai Essencia, for example, VA is openly encouraged. Small quantities of acetic acid are a natural by-product of the fermentation process. However, if the finished wine comes into prolonged contact with air, a bacteria known as Acetobactor causes a reaction between the alcohol in the wine and oxygen to produce markedly higher levels of acetic acid. An excess of such VA leads to the wine being spoilt. It is generally detected by the taster as an aroma of vinegar or nail polish remover (ethyl acetate is produced contemporaneously with an increase in acetic acid) and a sour, thin flavour on the palate. Such wines are described as having excessive volatility.

Volatility
An excess of volatile acidity.

Wine Press
A crushing device used to press grapes and drain away the grape juice from solids such as skins, pips, etc.

Yeast
An organism, either wild or cultured, that is a vital component of the fermentation process. Wine yeast "consumes" sugar as an energy source and the by-products of this activity are alcohol and carbon dioxide. This reaction is known as fermentation and the resulting liquid; wine. But you already know that don't you.

INDEX

Alkoomi Classic White 151
All Saints The Lyrebird range 187
Andrew Garret Shiraz 79
Andrew Garrett Pinot Noir
   Chardonnay N.V. 189
Ashton Hills Pinot Noir 124
Baileys "Founder Series" 187
Baileys "Gold Label" Muscat 187
Baileys "Warby Range" 187
Baileys "Winemakers Selection" 187
Baileys 1920's Block Shiraz 71
Baileys Shiraz (Formerly Classic
   Hermitage) 71
Bannockburn Chardonnay 159
Bannockburn Pinot Noir 124
Bannockburn Saignee 133
Bannockburn Shiraz 101
Basedows White Burgundy
   [Semillon] 160
Bests Great Western Bin O Shiraz . .102
Bests Great Western Cabernet
   Sauvignon 102
Bests Great Western Pinot
   Meunier 102
Bowen Estate Cabernet Sauvignon . . .72
Bowen Estate Shiraz 79
Briar Ridge Semillon 137
Briar Ridge Stockhausen Semillon . .138
Bridgewater Mill Millstone Shiraz . . .72
Bridgewater Mill Sauvignon Blanc . .152
Brokenwood Graveyard Vineyard
   Shiraz 80
Brokenwood Semillon 138
Brown Brothers Tarrango 133
Campbells "Merchant Prince"
   Rutherglen Muscat 187
Campbells Liqueur Muscat and
   Tokay 187
Cape Clairault "Clairault" 103
Cape Clairault Semillon Sauvignon
   Blanc 152
Cape Mentelle Cabernet Merlot
   'Trinders V/yard' 104
Cape Mentelle Cabernet
   Sauvignon 80
Cape Mentelle Chardonnay 161
Cape Mentelle Semillon\Sauvignon
   Blanc 153
Cape Mentelle Shiraz 80
Cape Mentelle Zinfandel 81
Capel Vale Baudin 103
Capel Vale Chardonnay 160
Capel Vale Riesling 144
Capel Vale Semillon/Sauvignon
   Blanc 152
Capel Vale Shiraz 103
Capel Vale Special Reserve
   "Frederick" Chardonnay 161
Cassegrain Chambourcin 104
Cassegrain Fromenteau
   Chardonnay 162
Chambers Rosewood Old Liqueur
   Muscat and Old Liqueur Tokay . .187
Chambers Rosewood Special
   Liqueur Tokay & Muscat 187
Chapel Hill Cabernet Sauvignon 81
Chapel Hill Shiraz 81
Charles Melton "Nine Popes" 81
Charles Melton Rosé of Virginia . . .134
Chateau Tahbilk Cabernet
   Sauvignon 82
Chateau Tahbilk Marsanne 138
Chateau Tahbilk Old Vines 72
Chateau Tahbilk Shiraz 82
Coldstream Hills "Reserve"
   Chardonnay 162
Coldstream Hills "Reserve" Pinot
   Noir 125
Coldstream Hills 'Reserve'
   Cabernet Sauvignon 104
Cope-Williams "Romsey" 190
Craiglee Shiraz 105
Cranswick Estate 179
Crawford River Riesling 144
Croser 190
Cullen Cabernet Merlot 105
Cullen Chardonnay 162
Cullen Sauvignon Blanc 163
Cullen Semillon/Sauvignon Blanc
   "Reserve" 163
Dalwhinnie Moonambel Cabernet . . .73
Dalwhinnie Moonambel Shiraz 73
De Bortoli Noble One Semillon 180
Delamere Pinot Noir 125
Delatite Devils River 105
Delatite Riesling 144
Diamond Valley Blue label Pinot
   Noir 125
Diamond Valley Estate 'White label'
   Pinot Noir 125
Domain Chandon Blanc de Blancs . .191
Domaine Chandon Blanc de Noirs .191

INDEX

Domaine Chandon Vintage Brut ...190
Elderton "Command" Shiraz 83
Evans & Tate Cabernet
    Sauvignon 106
Evans & Tate Chardonnay 163
Evans & Tate Semillon 164
Evans & Tate Shiraz [Previously
    labelled as Hermitage] 106
Evans & Tate WA Classic 153
Evans and Tate Merlot 106
Giaconda Cabernet
    Sauvignon\Merlot\Franc 107
Giaconda Chardonnay 164
Giaconda Pinot Noir 126
Goona Warra Cabernet Franc 107
Goonawarra Semillon 164
Goundrey Reserve Riesling 144
Goundrey Reserve Shiraz 107
Gramps Botrytis Semillon 180
Gramps Cabernet Merlot 108
Grant Burge Chardonnay 165
Grosset Gaia 108
Grosset Noble Riesling 180
Grosset Piccadilly Chardonnay 165
Grosset Polish Hill Riesling 145
Grosset Watervale Riesling 145
Hainault "Reserve" Pinot Noir 126
Hanging Rock "Macedon" 191
Hanging Rock Heathcote Shiraz 83
Hardy's Collection Beerenauslese
    Riesling 181
Hardys Eileen Hardy
    Chardonnay 165
Hardys Eileen Hardy Shiraz 83
Heggies Botrytis Riesling 181
Heggies Vineyard Cabernets 109
Henschke "Cyril Henschke"
    Cabernet Sauvignon 84
Henschke "Julius" Riesling 145
Henschke Hill of Grace 84
Henschke Mount Edelstone 84
Henschke Noble Rot Riesling 181
Henschke Semillon 165
Hollick Coonawarra 85
Hollick Ravenswood Cabernet
    Sauvignon 109
Houghton Cabernet Rosé 134
Houghton Show Reserve White
    Burgundy 153
Houghton White Burgundy 154
Howard Park Cabernet Sauvignon ..85
Howard Park Riesling 146
Hugo Cabernet Sauvignon 85
Hugo Shiraz 86
Huntington Estate Cabernet
    Merlot 109
Huntington Estate Cabernet
    Sauvignon 110
Ingoldby Cabernet Sauvignon 86
Jansz Cuvee Brut 192
Jasper hills Emily's Paddock Shiraz-
    Cabernet Franc 73
Jasper hills Georgia's Paddock
    Shiraz 73
Jim Barry "The Armagh" Shiraz 74
Katnook Sauvignon Blanc 154
Killawarra Brut 192
Knights Granite Hills Riesling 146
Lake's Folly Chardonnay 166
Lake's Folly Cabernet Sauvignon ...110
Leeuwin Estate Cabernet
    Sauvignon 111
Leeuwin Estate Chardonnay 166
Leeuwin Prelude Chardonnay 167
Lefroy Brook Chardonnay 167
Lenswood Vineyards Pinot Noir 126
Lenswood Vineyards Sauvignon
    Blanc 139
Leo Buring "Leonay" Eden Valley
    Riesling 146
Leo Buring "Leonay" Watervale
    Riesling 147
Leo Buring DR 505 Cabernet
    Sauvignon 86
Lillydale Cabernet Merlot 111
Lillydale Yarra Chardonnays 167
Lindemans Hunter River
    Chardonnay 168
Lindemans Hunter River Semillon ..139
Lindemans Hunter River Shiraz
    ["Burgundy"] 111
Lindemans Hunter River Steven
    Shiraz [Hermitage] 112
Lindemans Limestone Ridge
    Shiraz-Cabernet 112
Lindemans Tokay Solera WH2 187
Lindemans White Label Muscat
    Solera 1625 187
Main Ridge Cabernet Sauvignon ...112
Main Ridge Chardonnay 168
Main Ridge Pinot Noir 127
McAlister, The 113

INDEX

McWilliams "Elizabeth" Semillon . . .139
McWilliams "Lovedale" Semillon . . .140
McWilliams Barwang Cabernet
    Sauvignon 87
McWilliams Barwang Shiraz 87
Miranda Estate Golden Botrytis 182
Mitchell Watervale Riesling 147
Mitchelton Riesling 147
Montara Pinot Noir 127
Moorooduc Estate Cabernet
    Sauvignon 113
Moorooduc Estate Chardonnay 169
Moorooduc Estate Pinot Noir 128
Morris Liqueur Muscat and Tokay . .187
Morris Old Premium Liqueur
    Muscat and Tokay 187
Moss Wood Cabernet Sauvignon
    [Incl. Reserve] 114
Moss Wood Margaret River
    Semillon 169
Moss Wood Margaret River
    Semillon (Unwooded) 140
Mount Avoca Cabernet Sauvignon . . .88
Mount Avoca Sauvignon Blanc 155
Mount Langi Ghiran Cabernet
    Sauvignon/Merlot 89
Mount Langi Ghiran Shiraz 89
Mount Mary "Triolet" 141
Mount Mary 'Quintet' Cabernets . . .114
Mount Mary Pinot Noir 128
Mountadam "The Red" 88
Mountadam Cabernet Sauvignon 87
Mountadam Chardonnay 169
Mountadam Pinot Noir 128
Nicholson River Pinot Noir 129
Nicholson River
    Chardonnay 170
Oakridge "Reserve" Cabernet
    Sauvignon 115
Orlando "Jacaranda Ridge"
    (Coonawarra) Cabernet
    Sauvignon 89
Orlando "St Hugo" (Coonawarra)
    Cabernet Sauvignon 90
Orlando St Helga Riesling 148
Orlando St Hilary Chardonnay 170
Orlando Steingarten Riesling 148
Parker Coonawarra Estate "Terra
    Rossa First Growth" 90
Penfolds Bin 28 "Kalimna" 90
Penfolds Bin 389 Cabernet-Shiraz . . .91

Penfolds Bin 707 Cabernet
    Sauvignon 74
Penfolds Grange Hermitage 75
Penfolds Koonunga Hill Shiraz/
    Cabernet Sauvignon 115
Penfolds Magill Estate Shiraz 91
Penley Estate Coonawarra Cabernet
    Sauvignon 91
Petaluma Chardonnay 171
Petaluma Coonawarra 92
Petaluma Riesling 148
Peter Lehmann "Stonewell" Shiraz . . .92
Peter Lehmann Noble Semillon 182
Peter Lehmann Semillon 171
Peter Lehmann Shiraz 92
Peter Rumball Sparkling Shiraz 192
Pierro Chardonnay 171
Pierro Semillon/Sauvignon Blanc
    L.T.C 155
Pikes Cabernet Sauvignon 93
Pikes Riesling 149
Pikes Sauvignon Blanc 155
Pikes Shiraz 93
Pipers Brook Chardonnay 172
Pipers Brook Riesling 149
Plantagenet "Omrah" 141
Plantagenet Cabernet Sauvignon . . .115
Plantagenet Mount Barker
    Chardonnay 172
Plantagenet Shiraz 116
Preece Cabernets 116
Preece Chardonnay 172
Redbank Sally's Paddock 116
Riddoch Run Shiraz 93
Rochecombe Sauvignon Blanc 156
Rockford Alicante Bouschet Rosé . . .134
Rockford Black Shiraz 193
Rosemount "Diamond Label"
    Shiraz 94
Rosemount Balmoral Syrah
    [Shiraz] .75
Rosemount Diamond Label
    Chardonnay 173
Rosemount Roxburgh
    Chardonnay 173
Rosemount Show Reserve Cabernet
    Sauvignon 94
Rosemount Show Reserve
    Chardonnay 174
Rosemount Show Reserve
    Semillon 174

INDEX

Rothbury Hunter Semillon 141
Rothbury Reserve Shiraz 117
Saltram Classic Shiraz 117
Sandstone Cabernet Sauvignon 117
Sandstone Semillon 175
Schinus Rosé 134
Schinus Sauvignon Blanc 156
Scotchmans Hill Pinot Noir 129
Seaview Cabernet Sauvignon 95
Seaview Pinot Noir Chardonnay
    Vintage 193
Seppelt "Salinger" 195
Seppelt "Show" Sparkling Burgundy
    (Great Western) 194
Seppelt Black Label Cabernet
    Sauvignon 118
Seppelt Black Label Shiraz 118
Seppelt Chalambar Shiraz 118
Seppelt Dorrien Cabernet
    Sauvignon 95
Seppelt Fleur de Lys Premium
    Cuvee .193
Seppelt Great Western "St Peters"
    Shiraz .119
Seppelt Harper's Range Sparkling
    Burgundy 194
Seppelt Show Muscat and Show
    Tokay .187
Sevenhill Shiraz 95
Seville Estate Botrytis affected
    Riesling 182
Seville Estate Cabernet Sauvignon . .119
Seville Estate Shiraz 119
Sharefarmers Blend 120
Shaw & Smith Sauvignon Blanc . . .156
Sorrenberg Chardonnay 175
Sorrenberg Gamay 130
Stafford Ridge Sauvignon Blanc 156
Stonier's Reserve Chardonnay 175
Stoniers Reserve Pinot Noir 130
Taltarni "French Syrah" [Shiraz] 96
Taltarni Brut Tache 195
Taltarni Cabernet Sauvignon 96
Taltarni Pyrenees 135
Taltarni Rosé des Pyrenees 135
Tarrawarra Chardonnay 176
Thistle Hill Cabernet Sauvignon 97
Tim Knappstein Botrytis
    Riesling 183
Tim Knappstein Riesling 149
Tollana Botrytis Riesling 183

Tollana Eden Valley Riesling 150
Tollana TR222 Cabernet
    Sauvignon 97
Tyrrell's Old Winery Chardonnay . .176
Tyrrell's Vat 47 Pinot Chardonnay . .176
Tyrrell's Lost Block Semillon 141
Tyrrell's Old Winery Cabernet
    Merlot .120
Tyrrell's Vat 1 Semillon (confusingly
    labelled as "Riesling") 142
Vasse Felix Cabernet Sauvignon 120
Vasse Felix Classic Dry White 157
Vasse Felix Shiraz 121
Virgin Hills 121
Wendouree Cabernet Sauvignon 76
Wendouree Pressings 76
Wendouree Shiraz 77
Wendouree Shiraz Mataro 77
Wignalls Pinot Noir 130
Wilton Estate Botrytis Semillon 184
Wirra Wirra Sauvignon Blanc 157
Wolf Blass "Classic Shiraz"
    Brown Label 97
Wolf Blass Gold Label Riesling 150
Wyangan Estate Chardonnay 177
Wynns Coonawarra Cabernet
    Sauvignon 98
Wynns Coonawarra Hermitage 121
Wynns Coonawarra Riesling 150
Wynns John Riddoch Cabernet
    Sauvignon 78
Yalumba "D" 197
Yalumba Angus Brut 196
Yalumba Angus Brut Rose 196
Yalumba Cuvee One Prestige 196
Yalumba Family Reserve
    Chardonnay 177
Yalumba Family Reserve Shiraz 98
Yarra Ridge Botrytis Semillon 184
Yarra Ridge Chardonnay 178
Yarra Ridge Sauvignon Blanc 157
Yarra Yering Dry Red No2 99
Yarra Yering Dry red No 1 98
Yarra Yering Pinot Noir 131
Yeringberg "Yeringberg"
    (Formerly Cabernet) 122
Yeringberg "Yeringberg"
    [formerly Marsanne] 142
Yeringberg Pinot Noir 131
Zema Estate Cabernet Sauvignon . . .99
Zema Estate Shiraz 99

215

PERSONAL TASTING NOTES

PERSONAL TASTING NOTES

PERSONAL TASTING NOTES

PERSONAL TASTING NOTES

PERSONAL TASTING NOTES

PERSONAL TASTING NOTES

PERSONAL TASTING NOTES

PERSONAL TASTING NOTES